Dear Intrepid Adventurer,

Remember the last time an Indiana Jones movie came out? Let me refresh your memory.

George H. W. Bush became president; Pan Am Flight 103 blew up over Scotland; the Exxon Valdez supertanker spilled 11 million gallons into Alaska's Prince William Sound; Scott Adams's comic strip *Dilbert* debuted; Disney World opened; protesting students were suppressed in Beijing's Tiananmen Square; the first episode of *Seinfeld* aired; hurricane Hugo hammered the East Coast; and the Berlin Wall came crashing down.

What a year! It was 1989.

It was also the last time we saw an Indiana Jones adventure at the movies. In *Indiana Jones and the Last Crusade*, we see Indy and company ride off into the sunset—a proper ending to what was originally intended as a three-film series.

But Indy refused to die; he refused to hang up his fedora and lay aside his bullwhip, for which millions of longtime Indy fans are grateful. Saddled up for a fourth adventure, Indy rides again! This time, he's fighting the Soviets for possession of a priceless artifact, the Crystal Skull.

It's about time for his return, don't you agree?

—George Beahm

Indy and Marion narrowly escape from an explosive situation. (Indiana Jones Stunt Spectacular, Walt Disney World, Orlando, Florida)

Archaeology is the search for fact. *Not truth.* If it's truth you're interested in, Doctor Tyree's philosophy class is right down the hall.

So forget any ideas you've got about lost cities, exotic travel, and digging up the world. We do not follow maps to buried treasure, and "X" never, *ever,* marks the spot.

Seventy percent of all archaeology is done in the library. Research. Reading.

—Indiana Jones, from the original movie script
of *Indiana Jones and the Last Crusade*

INDIANA JONES

Off the Beaten Path

An Unofficial Expedition

GEORGE BEAHM

Illustrations by Tim Kirk

FOREWORD BY ARCHAEOLOGIST ERIC H. CLINE

HAMPTON ROADS
PUBLISHING COMPANY, INC.

Indiana Jones—Off the Beaten Path
An Unofficial Expedition

George Beahm

Hampton Roads Publishing Company, Inc.
1125 Stoney Ridge Road
Charlottesville, VA 22902

434-296-2772
fax: 434-296-5096
e-mail: hrpc@hrpub.com
www.hrpub.com

If you are unable to order this book from your local
bookseller, you may order directly from the publisher.
Call 1-800-766-8009, toll-free.

Library of Congress Cataloging-in-Publication Data

Beahm, George.
 Indiana Jones : off the beaten path : an unofficial expedition / George
Beahm.
   p. cm.
 Includes bibliographical references.
 Summary: "A behind-the-scenes look at the Indiana Jones movies and
television series. Explores the facts and myths surrounding the character,
introduces readers to a real archaeologist, and shows how they can 'become'
Indiana Jones"--Provided by publisher.
 ISBN-13: 978-1-57174-558-3 (6 x 9 tp : alk. paper)
 1. Indiana Jones films--History and criticism. 2. Jones, Indiana
(Fictitious character) I. Title.
 PN1995.9.I47B43 2008
 791.43'75--dc22

2007050875
ISBN 978-1-57174-558-3
10 9 8 7 6 5 4 3 2 1
Printed on acid-free paper in Canada

for my wife, Mary, indisputably
the #1 Indiana Jones fan in the world

◄ TABLE OF CONTENTS ►

Foreword, by archaeologist Dr. Eric H. Cline. . . . . **IX**

Cliffhanging with Indiana Jones: FAN-tastic Adventures! . . . . . . **XIII**

Part 1. The Fictional World of Indiana Jones

Fedora, Bullwhip, and Revolver: The Origins of Indiana Jones. **3**

Meet the Cast: Key Characters **7**

A Film-by-Film Look **17**

A Walk through the Twentieth Century: History with
  Indiana Jones, or *The Young Indiana Jones Chronicles* **33**

Part 2. Indiana Jones: Fact, Fiction, or Folklore?

Raiders of the Lost Ark: South America and Egypt, 1936 . . . . **57**

Indiana Jones and the Temple of Doom: China and India, 1935 . . . . **73**

Indiana Jones and the Last Crusade: Venice, Austria,
  and Alexandretta, 1938 . . . . **81**

Indiana Jones and the Kingdom of the Crystal Skull: 1950s **87**

Part 3. The Disney Connection and Dress for Success, Indiana Jones Style

Experiencing the Indiana Jones Adventure Worldwide **91**

Dressing and Looking the Part. **99**

Part 4. Ports of Call for the Intrepid: Locations by Movie

Raiders of the Lost Ark. **107**

Indiana Jones and the Temple of Doom **111**

Indiana Jones and the Last Crusade. **113**

Part 5. Archaeology

Field Notes on Archaeology **123**

Raiders of the Faux Ark, by Dr. Eric H. Cline **127**

Digging It: A Day in the Life of a Field Archaeologist. **137**

Fabled Places and Relics, Lost Cities, and Ancient Civilizations . . **145**

Archaeological Resources **153**

Part 6. General Resources **157**

Acknowledgments. **171**

The Members of This Expedition **173**

A façade of an ancient Aztec temple, located near the Indiana Jones Stunt spectacular (Walt Disney World, Orlando, Florida).

FOREWORD

by Eric H. Cline, George Washington University

Although I am a professional archaeologist, happily digging under the hot sun, eating dirt, trying to avoid being stung by scorpions every summer, and teaching classes at a university during the school year, I can honestly say that I've never had to escape from a large rolling rock, or run from poisonous darts, or find my way out of a snake-infested Egyptian tomb, or even climb out of my window to avoid students wanting to see me during office hours. And I am not alone—not one of my professional colleagues has ever had those experiences (except for perhaps the last one!). I did have a bullwhip once, but it was given to me as a birthday present, and it rarely saw action except on Halloween night.

Perhaps this is stating the obvious, but Indiana Jones is a Saturday afternoon matinee idol, not an archaeologist. In fact, he and Lara Croft, the Tomb Raider, make an ideal couple, for neither of them comes close to resembling a professional archaeologist—although at least he shows up to teach in a classroom every so often. I ask no more of him, however, than that he be entertaining each and every time I watch him—for that is all he is supposed to be. I even have a poster from *Raiders of the Lost Ark* in my university office. If, and when, students take my classes because of Indiana Jones, which they frequently do, I am happy that they have done so, for I can easily repair any misconceptions they have.

Without a doubt, the Indiana Jones films have had a major impact on the field of archaeology. Almost all of my students who take my Introduction to Archaeology class cite the films as one reason why they wanted to enroll in the class . . . and perhaps even to declare a major in archaeology. So, I have a little fun with them on the first day: After going through the syllabus and discussing what will be on the midterm and final exams, I then explain that I need to spend about ten minutes showing them a documentary on how not to do archaeology, so that we get things off on the proper foot right at the beginning of the semester.

I warn them that the documentary might be a bit boring, but that's how life is . . . and then I pop in *Raiders of the Lost Ark* and show the opening sequence, right up until the time he gets away from the large rolling rock, avoids the poisonous darts, jumps into the seaplane, and mutters something about hating snakes. The class laughs throughout the sequence, amused that they are not actually watching a documentary, but then I turn serious and spend a few more minutes explaining why what he is doing is not archaeology and tell them that we will spend the next fifteen weeks learning the proper way to do archaeology. It always gets the semester off to a good start.

To my mind, the Indiana Jones movies act as a catalyst for developing interests in proper archaeology, just as movies such as *Troy, Alexander,* and *300* serve to stimulate interest in ancient Greece despite the inaccuracies that Hollywood frequently interjects into the plots. Unlike false claims by pseudo-archaeologists, the Indiana Jones movies do not pretend to portray reality—no real archaeologist is actively searching for the Ark of the Covenant, Sankara stones, the Holy Grail, or a crystal skull with amazing powers. The movies do, however, demonstrate the constructive effect that pop culture can have on legitimate research: They provide a point of discussion and departure from which one can properly present archaeology. In short, they give me the opportunity to explain to my students why Indiana Jones is more an adventurer and treasure-seeker than a proper archaeologist, which is a subtle but necessary distinction, and to teach them what it is that archaeologists really do.

Personally, I hope that Hollywood will continue to make such movies and will continue to use real archaeologists and academics as consultants, for through such productions we can reach—and begin to teach—yet another segment of the world's population. Although the movies are more Hollywood fiction than fact, they create a greater public awareness of archaeology as a discipline and open doors to legitimate inquiries. And when it comes right down to it, these movies are fun. Saturday afternoon is meant for entertainment; we can always fix the misperceptions and inaccuracies on Monday morning.

Dr. Eric H. Cline at a summer dig in Megiddo, Israel

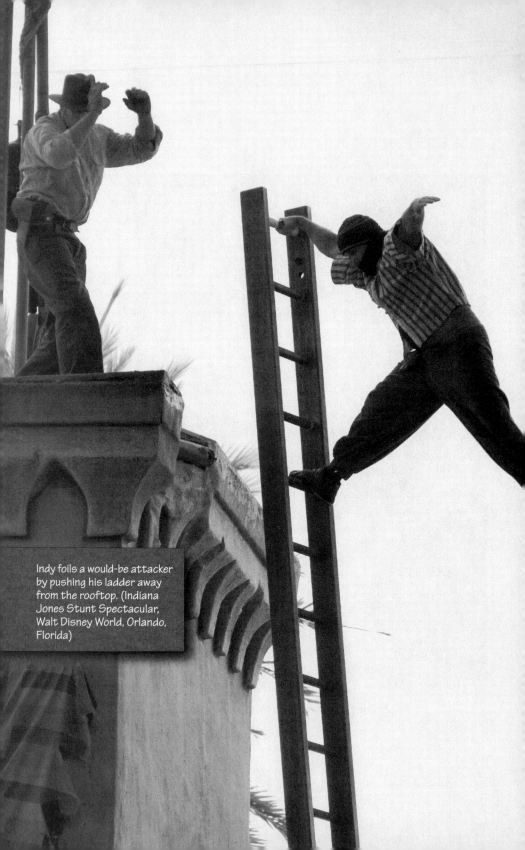

Indy foils a would-be attacker by pushing his ladder away from the rooftop. (Indiana Jones Stunt Spectacular, Walt Disney World, Orlando, Florida)

CLIFFHANGING WITH INDIANA JONES: FAN-TASTIC ADVENTURES!

Not *too* long ago, in our own galaxy, a great adventure took place. In 1981, in a story set in South America in 1936, a swashbuckling archaeologist named Dr. Indiana Jones made his debut in movie theaters worldwide—to instant acclaim. Wearing a battered fedora hat, leather jacket, khaki work shirt and matching pants, and patent leather boots, Dr. Jones carried a coiled bullwhip and a revolver for protection. Sporting a sly, knowing grin and several days' worth of stubble, Dr. Jones lives comfortably in two worlds: the sedate academic atmosphere at a New York college, where he teaches archaeology mostly to distracted lovesick coeds, and exotic ports the world over.

Imaginatively interpreted by veteran actor Harrison Ford, best known for his role as space smuggler Han Solo in *Star Wars,* Dr. Indiana Jones is a big lug who is always chasing someone . . . or being chased, as creator George Lucas has explained in numerous interviews over the years.

Welcome to the world of Dr. Indiana Jones, where anything can, and does, happen.

To date three films have appeared: *Raiders of the Lost Ark* (June 1981), *Indiana Jones and the Temple of Doom* (May 1984), and *Indiana Jones and the Last Crusade* (May 1989). Soon to be added to that list is *Indiana Jones and the Kingdom of the Crystal Skull* (May 2008).

Additionally, a television series titled *The Young Indiana Jones Chronicles* served up twenty-two feature-length installments, which allowed filmmaker George Lucas the opportunity to dish out appetizing educational fare in the form of palatable entertainment. In the series, the young Indiana Jones meets, and learns life's lessons from, the twentieth century's notable movers, shakers, and moneymakers, and of course also encounters some nefarious figures in the process.

There are also new stories told in comic books and novels, plus fan fiction on the Internet, but these don't provide the Indy fix most people are looking for. The average fan wants to visit his local theater, buy a large drink, cradle a tub of buttered popcorn on his lap, and, in that darkened room, see Indy larger than life on the silver screen as Lucas's THX sound system brings John Williams's magnificent score to full crescendo.

Why, you wonder, has Indy been gone from the screen so long? Well, there are two reasons.

Logistically, it was difficult to synchronize the schedules of Spielberg, Lucas, and Ford.

Then there was the problem of unsatisfactory screenplays. Though Frank Darabont's met with director Spielberg's approval, it didn't satisfy producer Lucas, to Darabont's frustration and outright indignation (a wasted year of his life, as he put it).

But the long drought will end on May 22, 2008, when the fourth film in the series, *Indiana Jones and the Kingdom of the Crystal Skull,* is released.

Doesn't that title have a nice ring to it? It sounds like a pulp adventure story, complete with gaudy, eye-catching covers and action-packed adventures!

Undoubtedly *the* most eagerly anticipated film in many years, *Indy 4* (as fans call it) will be a popcorn movie in the finest tradition of cliffhangers from the thirties and forties. This crowd-pleasing family film will have something for everyone: the return of Harrison Ford as Dr. Indiana Jones, older and undoubtedly wiser; the long-awaited return of the spunkiest heroine in the series, Marion Ravenwood, played by Karen Allen; and for the younger crowd, the popular Shia LaBeouf—beouf-cake, as it were. (Sadly, we won't see Indy's good friend and colleague Dr. Marcus Brody, played by the talented Denholm Elliott, who passed away in 1992.)

Not surprisingly, the moviegoing public has been eagerly seeking any morsel of information about Indy's latest adventure, but George Lucas has held his cards close to his chest. He knows that the film doesn't need to be hyped. He knows that moviegoers worldwide are looking forward to seeing their favorite hero shaken and stirred, pursuing and pursued, afflicted with snakes and other creepy-crawlers, and hell-bent on a mission despite dastardly foes. Though we may not know all the details, we can be sure that, in the end, Dr. Indiana Jones will triumph.

It's a message with great appeal in our troubled times of elusive terrorists and a war that seems like it'll never end (don't all wars seem that way?).

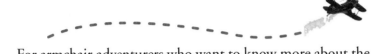

For armchair adventurers who want to know more about the world of Indiana Jones than can be found in official books or fan websites, this book goes well off the beaten path, and for good reason: Official books understandably tend to be hagiographic; for instance, you aren't going to find a negative word about *Temple of Doom* in any of them, though the movie should have been titled *Temple of Gloom*.

In this book, I pull no punches. I tell you all about the good, the bad, and the ugly. I never truckle. I tell the truth. Trust me. . . .

Modeled after my *Caribbean Pirates,* this book looks at fact and fiction through the lens of the Indiana Jones movies: What's based in truth, and what's Hollywood magic? This book also covers the Disney experience, notably the theme park ride at Disneyland and the Epic Stunt Spectacular at Disney World, with art by Tim Kirk, a veteran Imagineer who helped design the Disney-MGM Studio theme park and also designed the static exhibits of the Indy Jones encampments at both Disneyland and Walt Disney World. I even show you where to go to get outfitted in Indiana Jones garb, in case you *gotta* look the part. In addition, the book tells you about some of the world's most exotic ports of call where Indiana Jones has made an appearance, in both the real and fictional world. And, of course, it provides a wealth of resources for the adventurer who doesn't mind leaving the tour guide in the dust, so you can do a little exploring on your own. And I also introduce you to a *real* archaeologist, Dr. Eric H. Cline, who provides insights from his dual perspective as a professor in the classroom and a field archaeologist.

In short, this book is your passport to a world of adventure Indiana Jones style!

So grab your backpack and let's move out! As Marcus Brody exhorted Indy, Sallah, and Indy's father in *The Last Crusade:* "Follow me! I know the way!"

PART 1

The Fictional World of Indiana Jones

"WHIP-CRACKING ARCHAEOLOGIST INDIANA JONES HAS BEEN VOTED THE TOP MOVIE HERO OF ALL TIME BY READERS OF FILM MAGAZINE *TOTAL FILM*. DR. JONES, AN AMERICAN PROFESSOR OF ARCHAEOLOGY WHO TRAVELS AROUND THE WORLD SAVING PRECIOUS ARTIFACTS FROM NAZIS IN THE 1930S, HAS APPEARED IN THREE FILMS OVER THE LAST NINETEEN YEARS."

—BBC News, January 2001,
"Indiana Jones tops hero hot list"

A replica of Indiana Jones's diary. It is bound in cowhide and aged; the cover shows an ibis, the symbol of the Egyptian god Thoth. (Prop replica by Anthony Magnoli)

FEDORA, BULLWHIP, AND REVOLVER: THE ORIGINS OF INDIANA JONES

FADE IN

EXT. FILM STUDIO—DAY

A large sign reads: "Shady Films Studio"

CUT TO

INT. FILM STUDIO OFFICE

An EXECUTIVE is seated behind an oversized oak table. He has three of his bored minions flanking him. Elegantly framed movie posters decorate the wall. The man facing them is a nervous filmmaker and he's betting that his new idea will blow them away.

The EXECUTIVE looks bored. This is a pitch meeting, one of thousands he's heard in his long career as the head of Shady Films Studio. He's heard everything under the sun but wants something new, fresh, exciting! He leans forward in anticipation, hoping for the best.

EXECUTIVE

Okay, what have you got for me?

FILMMAKER

There's an adventurous archaeologist named Indiana Smith! He lives in New York City and he's a playboy. He doesn't spend much time in the classroom because he's typically running around the world finding lost artifacts. That's how he finances his expensive lifestyle in Manhattan. We're thinking Tom Selleck to play the lead.

THE EXECUTIVE leans back and sighs loudly. Clearly, he's underwhelmed.

EXECUTIVE

Don't like the name. Don't like the playboy aspect. Don't like New

York City as his home. Everybody's shooting there. Besides, isn't Tom tied up in contracts on *Magnum P.I.*? They aren't going to let him go.

Got anything *else?*

Actually, those were the initial thoughts of George Lucas when he conceived of the adventurous archaeologist. (And, no, that's probably not how he pitched it, but you get the idea. By the time he pitched it, with himself and Spielberg at the helm, every studio executive was probably foaming at the mouth to make a bid for it.)

After discussions with partner Steven Spielberg, George's vision substantially changed, and for the better. The main character would be named Indiana Jones. He wouldn't be a playboy in New York City. Instead, he'd be a solidly middle-class archaeology professor at a New York college. And Harrison Ford, a one-time carpenter whom Lucas hired for *American Graffiti* and, more famously, for *Star Wars,* would be cast in the pivotal role.

Conceived as popcorn movies, the Indiana Jones series would be pure entertainment, suitable for the whole family, and reintroducing filmgoers to the classic short serials that were mainstays in the 1930s and '40s. These black-and-white films were shown in installments before the main feature. Each film ended in a cliffhanger, a moment that promised certain, inescapable death to the hero . . . but, somehow, *the hero escapes!* Unfortunately, viewers had to wait a maddening week until the next Saturday when they came back to the theater to find out just *how* the hero managed to pull off the impossible, which is why they were aptly named cliffhangers.

Lucas was initially concerned about casting Harrison Ford because he felt he would become too closely identified with his films. Harrison proved to be the perfect fit, however: a leading man in the best traditions of Hollywood, a likeable guy who knows his place in the world and can take care of himself. Indy's a born leader. He's self-assured, intelligent, and has a great sense of humor. He's got a disarming lopsided grin on a ruggedly handsome face that has aged well over the years.

Can *you* think of anyone who would be better suited for the role of Indy than Harrison Ford? I can't.

The Indiana Jones movie formula is classic in its simplicity. As George Lucas explained, Indiana Jones is either chasing someone or being chased. It's pure action adventure, *the* key ingredient in a popcorn film, which is pure escapism. The movie's a visual roller-coaster ride. Have the viewer hang on for dear life and always have him wondering, "What's going to happen next?" Action, action! And more action! Pile it on!

Add to the mix a great cast. The bad guys are *really* bad (Nazis, Thuggee worshippers, and other nefarious sorts). The good guys are *really* good (Indy, Sallah, Dr. Marcus Brody). And the dames are *sometimes* in distress: spunky Marion Ravenwood can take care of herself, but Willie Scott grates as she screams her head off far too often, and Dr. Elsa Schneider is the ice queen who thaws under the combined wattage of the Drs. Jones (father and son).

The first movie, titled simply *Raiders of the Lost Ark,* hit screens worldwide in 1981. Looking back, Steven Spielberg explained (in an introduction to *Raiders of the Lost Ark: The Illustrated Screenplay*) that the movie's production was no easy feat:

> Casting commenced in February 1980, and shooting began in June. After 73 production days, 7,000 live snakes, 500 Arab extras, 11,000 shots, 300,000 feet of film exposed in four countries and across three continents, we were back in California watching Johnny Carson.

When *Raiders of the Lost Ark* exploded on movie screens worldwide, a new action hero was born. That rare commodity among Hollywood properties—a critical and financial success that becomes a film franchise—Indiana Jones, in his first adventure, gets the girl, recovers the long-lost treasure, and assumes his rightful place as the greatest action hero in Hollywood history.

In 1984, Lucas started using the line, "If adventure has a name . . . it must be Indiana Jones."

In 2008, that line *still* holds true.

Welcome back, Dr. Jones!

Indy attempts to steal the Golden Idol of Fertility in a pivotal scene reenacted from the first movie. (Indiana Jones Stunt Spectacular, Walt Disney World, Orlando, Florida)

MEET THE CAST:
KEY CHARACTERS

Let's face it, if you don't love the characters in a movie, what you've got is 120 minutes of bored viewers who don't give a rat's patootie whether the characters live or die. But if the producer and director have done their jobs, you're on the edge of your seat every time one of the good guys is in mortal danger, and you're loudly booing the bad guys when they appear on the screen.

The casting for the Indiana Jones movies is excellent. I have a bone to pick with a couple of the choices—well, Willie Scott, to name one—but that's more the fault of the screenwriter, not the actress in question. (From the footage of the bonus material in the Indy Jones DVD set, it's clear that Kate Capshaw is a real trouper. She'll do what she must to bring her character to life, but she was hamstrung by an ill-conceived script from Willard Huyck and Gloria Katz that stereotyped, instead of fleshing out, her character.)

Obviously, the cast of the four Indiana Jones movies is too extensive to include them all, so let me restrict my comments to some of the key characters, whom I discuss in alphabetical order, starting with the plucky heroine from the first and fourth films, Karen Allen.

ALLEN, KAREN (Marion Ravenwood; *Raiders, Crystal Skull*). Marion Ravenwood is the love interest. She's the daughter of Professor Abner Ravenwood, who taught Indy archaeology at the University of Chicago. According to Marion, her father characterized Indy as "his favorite bum" and loved him as if he were his own son, but there was an eventual falling-out, and Abner and Indy never had an opportunity to reconcile their differences before Abner passed away. (Indy had been so out of touch that he didn't know his mentor had died, for which he repeatedly apologizes to Marion.)

Indy protects Marion Ravenwood in a marketplace while villagers
(extras picked from the audience) look on with trepidation. (Indiana
Jones Stunt Spectacular, Walt Disney World, Orlando, Florida)

When we first meet Marion, she is running the Raven Saloon, a bar in
the remote, snow-swept mountains of Tibet; she has retreated from so-
called civilization to lick her wounds and mend her broken heart—broken,
of course, by Indy, who she claims took advantage of her some years ago—
a viewpoint Indy contests.

Marion's memories of Indy are understandably negative. Young and in
love, she fell hard for him and now harbors deep resentment. But when he
comes back into her life, searching for a medallion necessary to locate the
Lost Ark of the Covenant, he charms her once again. After he saves her
life, she returns the favor. It's clear that these two star-crossed lovers are
destined to be together. By turns feisty and compliant, combative and
accommodating, she's the *perfect* girlfriend for Indy. The screen chemistry
is palpable and, unlike the other female protagonists in the series, Marion
is no shrinking violet, no helpless, screaming dame. *This* one shows backbone, and a lot of it. Two thumbs way up for her memorable performance

in the first film. And, Karen, welcome back! We missed you! (In a bonus disc on the DVD set of Indy Jones movies, Steven Spielberg rightly cites her "spunk" and calls her a "firebrand." So true!)

BLANCHETT, CATE (Irina Spalko, *Crystal Skull*). In reprising her role as Marion Ravenwood in the fourth film, Karen Allen requires a worthy opponent. Enter Cate Blanchett, a screen veteran who has twice played Queen Elizabeth I and also Lady Galadriel in *The Lord of the Rings*, among other notable roles. Think catfight with Cold War overtones. An über-chick who recalls the female Terminator in *T-3*, Blanchett's character will likely be cold, merciless, and perhaps a bit manly. As Spielberg told her on the set one day, "I've got a few macho things for you to do today." Expect her to kick Indy's butt—and maybe Karen Allen's, as well. In her role as a formidable Russian interrogator, Cate will be like vodka: a distilled essence of a uniquely foreign spirit with a distinctive but memorable taste.

CAPSHAW, KATE (Wilhelmina Scott, *Temple of Doom*). Mrs. Steven Spielberg plays "Willie" Scott, a renowned American singer who gets swept up in Indy's adventure when he meets Chinese gangster Lao Che at the Obi Wan bar in Shanghai.

A reluctant adventuress who finds herself enduring a host of creepy, crawly critters (from bugs to snakes), her role—as a world-wise and travel-weary city girl who eventually finds herself in the forbidding Pankot palace—lacks the innate charm of the first Indy heroine, Marion Ravenwood, who has more personality and character.

Then, too, there is the matter of personal chemistry. In sharp contrast to Marion's combustible relationship with Indy, the faux heat between Willie and Indy is lackluster and doesn't convince. It looks and feels like acting, when it should look and feel like the real thing: true love, the *real* Holy Grail for us mere mortals.

Her scenes with Indy substituted comical romantic scenes for passion, which may have been what Lucas and Spielberg intended. But it's no improvement over the give-and-take relationship between Marion and Indy that we enjoyed in the first movie.

The fact is that the audience loved how Karen Allen portrayed Marion Ravenwood, and hoped to see her again. (We got our wish, but not in time for the second, or even third, Indy movie. Fortunately, the fourth proved to be the charm.)

CONNERY, SEAN (Professor Henry Jones, *Last Crusade*). In the role of Indy's father, Connery—a screen legend best known as British Secret Service agent 007 with a license to kill—comes into this movie with a license to thrill . . . and charm.

Though the age difference between Connery and Ford would realistically preclude their being father and son, audiences eagerly overlooked the chronological oddity and warmly embraced the crusty Professor Henry Jones. It is Connery's seamless portrayal as Indy's father that elevates this otherwise great adventure film to a heartwarming story as well—of a son also searching, and finding, his own Holy Grail, an elusive relationship with his father that needed closure. Or, as Indy elaborated to his father in one of the quiet moments in the third movie, "We didn't talk. We never talked. . . . It was just the two of us, Dad. It was a lonely way to grow up. For you, too. If you had been an ordinary, average father like the other guys' dads, you'd have understood that. . . . What you taught me was that I was less important to you than people who had been dead for five hundred years in another country. And I learned it so well that we've hardly spoken for twenty years."

It is this touching relationship between an estranged father and son that makes the movie so memorable; the quest for the actual Grail cup is clearly a secondary concern.

Connery's on-screen relationship with Denholm Elliott also catches fire. We get the sense that they are lifelong friends who would do anything for each other. They clearly respect each other. They are peers and share a relationship that stretches across many years.

Unfortunately, by the time casting began for the fourth film, Connery had announced his retirement as an actor. Consequently, we will never see Connery reprise his memorable role as Indy's father. Connery, a superb actor, left at the top of his game. Would it have been too much to ask for him to give us one more great performance as Professor Henry Jones?

DAVIES, JOHN-RHYS (Sallah; *Raiders, Last Crusade*). An Egyptian, Sallah is one of many friends Indy can call on around the world. Sallah, though, can credit his good fortune and long life to the fact that if it's a choice between Indy or him facing a dangerous situation, he quickly offers the opportunity for Indy to go first. That doesn't detract from

Sallah's courage, however, as he often takes chances and puts himself at risk, but not needlessly so, since he's a canny character.

Expertly played by John-Rhys Davies, the character Sallah is steadfast, trustworthy, and always willing to lend a hand. (Davies, as Sallah, also lends a hand as a tour guide for the Indiana Jones thrill ride in Disneyland. He offers helpful hints to riders who are about to go on the ride of their lives.)

DOODY, ALISON (Dr. Elsa Schneider, *Last Crusade*). Like Dr. Belloq, Dr. Schneider—an Austrian historian who isn't bookish-looking, but admittedly delectable as a tall, leggy blonde—harbors divided allegiances. On one hand, she willingly plays up to the Nazis, with whom she's reluctantly allied herself to get what she wants: a chance to find the legendary Holy Grail. On the other, she's torn between the two Joneses, father and son, but ends up preferring the younger version, closer to her own age.

Despite her Nazi affiliation, Elsa falls hard for Indy, and the feeling is reciprocated. In a pivotal scene, Elsa is asked to choose the Grail cup for rich collector/Nazi sympathizer Walter Donovan. She does so, but shows her true colors by deliberately, knowingly picking a false Grail cup, which takes Donovan's life. Similarly, she's concerned when Indy is forced to make a choice among the numerous Grail cups, but he chooses . . . *wisely.*

An engaging and likeable character—if you can overlook her minor character flaw, the tiny blemish of being allied with the Nazis—Elsa's life, at movie's end, hangs in the balance, literally. She need only reach up to grab Indy's hand and be pulled to safety out of the crevasse that opened up beneath her, but with her other hand, she can barely touch the rim of the Grail cup, and she must choose between it and Indy's hand.

"I would have done anything to get it," she told Indy earlier. And, unfortunately, she lives up to these words. The wide-eyed look, her face lit up by the prospect of owning the legendary Grail cup, foreshadows her choice. In the end, she chose . . . *poorly.*

ELLIOTT, DENHOLM (Dr. Marcus Brody; *Raiders, Last Crusade*). Marcus will be sorely missed in the fourth film. A much more conservative version of Indiana Jones, Marcus doesn't mind a taste of adventure, though he *does* tend to stick out like a sore thumb. In *Last Crusade,* for instance, he's hopelessly lost at a railroad station in Egypt, only to be recognized and rescued by Sallah. As Indy says to his father, "You know Marcus. He got lost once in his own museum!"

Marcus is a memorable character who adds the necessary comic relief, in addition to being Indy's peer. The chemistry between Marcus and Indy is palpable. But alas, when Brody rides off into the sunset with Indy and company in *Last Crusade,* it's the last time we will see him, because Elliott passed away in 1992.

FORD, HARRISON (Indiana Jones, all four films). Initially reluctant to cast Ford in yet another epic film series, creator George Lucas screened other actors, but the search proved elusive.

It was Steven Spielberg who wisely suggested Harrison Ford. The suggestion produced a long, weary sigh from George Lucas, who in a clip on a bonus disc for the Indy Jones DVD set explained, "He's been in two of my movies. I don't want him to be my Bobby De Niro. I don't want to have every movie I make star Harrison."

To his credit, Spielberg prevailed. "George and I had tested a lot of potential Indiana Joneses: from Tim Matheson to Peter Coyote to Tom Selleck." And because the screen test with Selleck was spot-on, Lucas and Spielberg initially pursued him, but it was not to be. Once they expressed an interest in him, the television producers that had Selleck committed long-term to *Magnum P.I.* refused to release him.

Back to square one.

In a climactic scene, Marion Ravenwood waits anxiously for Indy to remove the chockblock from the plane's wheels as they try to escape to safety. (Indiana Jones Stunt Spectacular, Walt Disney World, Orlando, Florida)

"Well, what are we going to do now?" mused Lucas.

"What about Harrison?" responded Spielberg.

It was, in the end, the best possible choice. Imagine Han Solo gone legit: a card-carrying professorial sort who, when he's not lecturing to dewy-eyed coeds in class, finds himself in the hairiest situations imaginable.

Named after Lucas's dog Indiana (an Alaskan malamute), the character is depicted in the original concept drawings by comic book artist Jim Steranko as a rock-jawed, tough guy—a pulp hero from the thirties or forties. But screenwriter Lawrence Kasdan fleshed out the character and humanized him, made him a likeable galoot, the kind of good guy you'd instantly warm to.

The character of Indiana Jones was born and, in short order, Harrison Ford would come to own the character of Indiana Jones to such an extent that it's unthinkable anyone would even attempt to follow in his footsteps. (It reminds one of Sean Connery as James Bond in the movies. There were other 007s but none with his flair, his dry wit, and his British charm. Imitated but never equaled, much less surpassed.)

Indy's got a few more adventures in him, and I hope Lucas and Spielberg go back to the drawing board and dream up a fifth movie, even if it's got a hokey title like the fourth movie.

FREEMAN, PAUL (Dr. Rene Belloq, *Raiders*). We meet this suave but slimy French archaeologist in the first movie. After risking life and limb to acquire the golden idol of fertility, Indy barely escapes . . . just in time for Belloq to take it from him, under the watchful eyes of a local South American tribe who speaks Hovitos, which Indy does not.

Charming in his own way, Belloq regrets (but not *too* much) having to do business with the Nazis, seeing the evil regime as a means to an end: The goose-stepping Aryans finance a dig near Cairo, Egypt, where Belloq hopes to recover the Lost Ark of the Covenant. (Once again, Indy discovers it first, only to have Belloq take it from him.)

Though Belloq gets his comeuppance, he's a formidable nemesis for Indy. They share a passion for antiquities, but Indy has a broad streak of morality that his French counterpart does not—an attribute that makes all the difference. Belloq, consumed by greed, meets a just end. Indy, of course, lives to see another day . . . and another adventure.

LaBEOUF, SHIA (Matt Dutton, *Crystal Skull*). As the youngest member of the cast, Shia was given the honor of formally announcing at the MTV Video Music Awards in 2007 the official title of the fourth Indy adventure, *Indiana Jones and the Kingdom of the Crystal Skull.*

Speculation is that Shia plays Indy's son, and that his mother is Marion Ravenwood. If so, this makes sense because it's hard to imagine Indy Jones falling for just *any* woman. Marion is cut from the same cloth Indy is: She's tough, resourceful, and intelligent but also a romantic and an optimist at heart with a great sense of humor.

Keeping in mind that Harrison Ford is sixty-six and nearly two decades have elapsed between the third and fourth films, it's necessary to inject new, young blood in this film franchise to get the attention of young viewers, so Shia (a rising star) is the bridge between two generations of fans.

I'm looking forward to seeing Shia racing on a motorcycle through the streets of a college campus with Indy hanging on for dear life.

LACEY, RONALD (Major Arnold Toht, *Raiders*). A Nazi henchman, Lacey's character is presumably a member of the feared Gestapo. Though this wonderful actor speaks only fourteen lines of dialogue, he's a scene-stealer who shows that actions speak louder than words.

At the time he was cast, this veteran actor, unable to find work, was agenting to pay the bills. Fortunately, he was cast in this small but memorable role. He appears, at first, to be an innocuous person, almost harmless, but looks can be deceiving, can't they?

Toht makes his appearance early in the first film, entering Marion Ravenwood's bar. Flanked by a nasty bunch of thugs, Toht is dismissed by Marion, who nonchalantly blows smoke in his face, as he coughs in obvious discomfort. We, too, perceive Toht as essentially harmless, but like Marion, we soon see his true colors. From the bar's fireplace, Toht extracts a poker with a glowing orange tip hissing with heat. He draws it near Marion's face. She now realizes she's dealing with someone who has no compunction about torturing her for information; more to the point, he would probably relish the opportunity. Quickly dropping her tough-broad persona, Marion eagerly offers to tell him everything. Toht, thinking of past similar scenarios, grins knowingly and responds, "I know you will. . . ."

In another scene, Toht, flanked by guards, enters the tent where Dr. Belloq and Marion Ravenwood have been drinking and are slightly inebriated. The music rises to a crescendo and we fear the worst for Marion, whose wide-eyed look shows how afraid she is of what he might do. He takes a curious implement made of three pieces of black wood, linked by chains, and handles it casually . . . a torture instrument? No. It's actually something else.

PHOENIX, RIVER (the teenage Indiana Jones, *Last Crusade*). In the setup story, we see young Indy on a Boy Scout excursion, where he runs across a dastardly gang who seek, and find, the Cross of Coronado. Indy temporarily rescues it from their clutches. He leads the plunderers on a wild goose chase, until he's derailed by the local sheriff.

The late River Phoenix is outstanding as the young Indiana Jones. Harrison Ford, in fact, pointed out that River Phoenix was the actor who most resembled him when he was that age. (Ford also cast River Phoenix as his son in *The Mosquito Coast*.)

It would have been great to see River Phoenix in the television series *The Young Indiana Jones Chronicles,* but it was not to be.

PURI, AMRISH (Mola Ram, *Temple of Doom*). A worthy nemesis who has heart, Mola, high priest of a Thuggee cult, is a bad guy par excellence. As high priest, he oversees the human sacrificial ceremonies witnessed by members of his bloodthirsty cult. Even without his ceremonial raiment on, Mola Ram exudes pure evil.

He almost gets the better of Indy—again, getting to the heart of the matter—but is finally bested and falls to his death, where he is devoured by crocodiles.

In a great performance from one of Indy's most formidable nemeses, actor Amrish Puri pulls off the role with brio . . . and a certain creepiness that's in character with the movie, which is pretty high on the gross-o-meter.

QUAN, JONATHAN KE (KE HUY QUAN) (Short Round, *Temple of Doom*). We first meet Quan, Indy's pint-sized sidekick in *Temple of Doom*, as he drives up in a Duisenberg outside Club Obi Wan in Shanghai. He then rockets off with Indy and Willy hanging on for dear life.

An engaging, resourceful, and loyal sidekick to father-figure Indy, Quan plays his role to perfection and is a bright light in an otherwise dark film that divided critics; some liked it, but a significant number did not, which is unusual for this film franchise.

Interestingly, Quan went to the casting call with his older brother in tow, hoping to get him to audition. But the casting director's eyes were on the younger Quan, who fit the bill perfectly, as he kept coaching his brother.

A great performance from a child actor, Quan is a natural. Or as Spielberg put it, "Just about the most gifted newcomer . . . I have ever worked with."

A FILM-BY-FILM LOOK

For too many years, if you wanted to see the movies, you had to fire up the VHS tape recorder/player because that was the only alternative. Happily, that changed in 2003 when Paramount Pictures issued a handsome boxed set of the first three films and a bonus disc, with all the footage digitally mastered to enhance the sound and picture quality.

For older fans who remember seeing *Raiders of the Lost Ark* on the movie screen, these outstanding versions are not only blasts from the past but eminently rewatchable, especially on large screen televisions with add-on speakers. (I watch mine on a forty-two-inch Panasonic plasma with a Bose sound system. It looks and sounds great!)

For new fans, these movies hold up very well indeed and, because they're set in the thirties, they don't have a dated feel as do movies set in our time. (Look at *Saturday Night Fever,* which came out in 1977. Doesn't

it look and feel old? But the first Indy film, which came out in 1981, still looks new and fresh and is great fun to watch repeatedly.)

Now, of course, Paramount will have to reissue this set with all four films and new bonus material, which gives us something to look forward to. Expect the DVD of movie #4 in the September-October 2008 timeframe.

Note: The DVDs are available in two flavors: widescreen and fullscreen. Widescreen is the preferred format, since it shows the movie without cropping, whereas fullscreen (designed for a conventionally sized television set) uses the odious "pan and scan" technique that crops out the sides of the picture frame.

RAIDERS OF THE LOST ARK

Release date: June 12, 1981
Running time: 115 minutes
Soundtrack: John Williams
Box office take (domestic): $242 million
Oscar wins: Best Art Direction, Set Decoration; Best Effects, Visual Effects; Best Film Editing; Best Sound. (Also nominated for Best Cinematography; Best Director; Best Music, Original Score; Best Picture.)
Major cast:
Harrison Ford as *Indiana Jones*
Karen Allen as *Marion Ravenwood*
Paul Freeman as *Dr. Rene Belloq*
Ronald Lacey as *Major Arnold Toht*
John Rhys-Davies as *Sallah*
Denholm Elliott as *Dr. Marcus Brody*

SYNOPSIS

Archaeology professor and part-time adventurer Indiana Jones is persuaded by army intelligence officers to find—before the Nazis do—the Ark of the Covenant, which Hitler wants to exploit as a military weapon. Financed by the Germans, an archaeological dig near Cairo, led by Dr. Rene Belloq, is close to discovering the Ark, but it remains elusive until

An artifact from Tec'na'al, the site Indy explored before
finding the lost temple of the Chachapoyan warriors
in the first movie. (Prop replica by Anthony Magnoli)

Indiana Jones shows up with the headpiece of Ra, which discloses the Ark's exact location on site.

Will Indy manage to avoid the clutches of the dastardly Nazis? Will Dr. Rene Belloq get his just rewards? Will Hitler ever get his hands on the Ark of the Covenant? Will Indy and Marion's relationship survive the stress of being business partners? And does the U.S. government keeps its promise to Indy and return the Ark to him after their "top men" have finished working on it?

CRITICS' CORNER

Rotten Tomatoes (www.rottentomatoes.com) rating: critics, 95%; fans, 98%. NOTE: This heavily trafficked website polls its audience of critics and fans for ratings. The figures cited gauge a movie's popularity with this audience.

George Beahm: Ranked #48 in terms of box office dollars (not adjusted for inflation), this movie is what Hollywood is all about: big budget, family entertainment, a popcorn movie that reminds us why we go to the movies in the first place—pure escapism, the equivalent of a roller-coaster ride at a theme park. Seamless in every way, this movie is pitch-perfect. It's hard to imagine anyone coming up with another action-adventure movie that will equal it in terms of overall excellence. The gold standard, this movie came out in 1981 and remains unchallenged. That's how good it is. Bottom line: A+.

Roger Ebert *(Chicago Sun-Times)*: It "plays like an anthology of the best parts from all the Saturday matinee serials ever made. . . . The movie is just plain fun. . . . Harrison Ford is the embodiment of Indiana Jones— dry, fearless, and as indestructible as a cartoon coyote. . . . It's a Boy's Own Adventure, a whiz-bang slamarama, a Bruised Forearm movie (you squeeze the arm of your date every time something startles you). It's done with a kind of heedless joy."

Stephen Klain *(Variety)*: "Raiders of the Lost Ark is the stuff that raucous Saturday matinees at the local Bijou once were made of, a crackerjack fantasy-adventure that shapes its pulp sensibilities and cliffhanging serial origins into an exhilarating escapist entertainment that will have . . . summer audiences in the palm of its hand. . . . Steeped in an exotic atmosphere of lost civilizations, mystical talismans, gritty mercenary adventurers, Nazi arch-villains, and ingenious death at every turn, the film is largely patterned on the serials of the 1930s, with a large added dollop of Edgar Rice Burroughs."

John Nesbit (CultureCartel.com): "Watching *Raiders of the Lost Ark* again on the big screen I was again reminded how summer films were once thoroughly entertaining and fulfilling. Spielberg retains respect for the audience with his impeccable technique and supplying nonstop action with good exposition, some memorable characters, great stunt work, and good special effects for the time."

Christopher Null (Filmcritic.com): "You'd have to be a heathen to argue with the fact that *Raiders of the Lost Ark* stands as the best action-adventure movie ever made."

Jimmy Summers (Boxoffice.com): "*Raiders of the Lost Ark* is a wonderful movie. The good news for exhibitors is that it's also one of those roller-coaster-like movies that people will be lining up for again and again. And because word of mouth should be the best since *Star Wars* and *Rocky*, and since critics and the general media have been giving the adventure more attention than a publicist ever could hope for, splashy advertising shouldn't be too necessary."

COMMENTS FROM THE CAST AND CREW

Film director **Steven Spielberg**: "I said I wanted to do a James Bond film. United Artists approached me after *Sugarland Express* and asked me to do a film for them. I said, 'Sure, give me the next Bond film.' But they said they couldn't do that. Then George said he had a film that was even better than a James Bond. It was called *Raiders of the Lost Ark,* and it was about this archaeological adventurer who goes searching for the Ark of the Covenant. When he mentioned it would be like the old serials and that the guy would wear a soft fedora and carry a bullwhip, I was completely hooked. George said, 'Are you interested?' and I said, 'I want to direct it,' and he said, 'It's yours.'" *(George Lucas: The Creative Impulse)*

Filmmaker **George Lucas** on the character of Indiana Jones: "He has to be a person we can look up to. We're doing a role model for little kids, so we have to be careful. We need someone who's honest and true and trusting." (from *Skywalking* by Dale Pollock)

Actor **Harrison Ford** on his character of Indiana Jones: "He's an archaeologist and a professor of archaeology. At the same time, he is an adventurer unconstrained by the usual niceties of the academic world. He is a swashbuckling type, but he has human frailties, fears, and money problems. He teaches, but I wouldn't describe him as an intellectual. He does brave things, but I wouldn't call him a hero. He's just in there with a bullwhip to keep the world at bay." (LucasFilm Fan Club #7, interview conducted by Dan Madsen and John S. Davis)

INDIANA JONES AND THE TEMPLE OF DOOM

Release date: May 23, 1984
Running time: 118 minutes
Soundtrack: John Williams
Box office take (domestic): $179 million
Oscar win: Best Effects, Visual Effects. (Also nominated for Best Music, Original Score.)
Major cast:
Harrison Ford as *Indiana Jones*
Kate Capshaw as *Wilhelmina "Willie" Scott*
Jonathan Ke Quan (Ke Huy Quan) as *Short Round*
Amrish Puri as *Mola Ram*
Roshan Seth as *Chattar Lal*
Philip Stone as *Captain Phillip Blumburtt*
Roy Chiao as *Lao Che*

SYNOPSIS

In this movie, unfortunately, anything goes. Jumping from the frying pan to the fire, so to speak, Indy and company narrowly escape the clutches of an evil Chinese gangster, Lao Che, in Shanghai only to find themselves in darkest India, where a village elder convinces Indy to recover the sacred Sivalinga stone, which turns out to be no easy task. Mola Ram, a maniacal and bloodthirsty high priest for a Thuggee cult, has enslaved the local village's children, bewitched the young maharajah of the Pankot palace, and relishes ripping throbbing hearts out of his victims, who are ceremoniously sacrificed to Kali, the bloodthirsty Indian goddess. Indy finds himself challenged on several fronts: He must not lose heart (literally); he must retrieve the sacred stone from the Thuggees; he must keep Willie and Short Round alive; and, finally, he has to free the enslaved children and get everyone safely back to the local village. A tall order, even for Indy!

Though the film was predictably a box office smash hit because fans would see this movie no matter what, and although numerous reviewers praised it as a different kind of story from the first one, the fact remained that for most viewers, this gratuitously dark movie struck a raw nerve with its images of child slavery, gross-out meals, whippings, human sacrifice, hearts torn out of victims, immolation, insects galore, a constantly screaming heroine (annoying in the extreme), and . . . well, the list goes on and on. This movie struck many filmgoers as dark, depressing, and hardly escapist fare fit for family entertainment. (What kind of person would *enjoy* watching children being chained, whipped, and enslaved?)

Although there is much to enjoy—Indy's encounter with Lao Che, the unbelievable mine car chase scene, and the riveting scene with Indy cutting the bridge while he's still standing on it—the fact remains that there's much to make the viewer wince, and needlessly so. (The film, as a result, prompted the MPAA to institute a new rating, PG-13.)

It is, and will likely remain, the least favorite of the Indiana Jones movies: a promising film flawed by its initial premise, one that, as Spielberg explained, was intentionally dark by design, as originally envisioned by George Lucas. In *The Cinema of George Lucas,* Spielberg

There's much to see while waiting in line for a ride. Here are some artifacts crated up and ready for shipment. (Indiana Jones Adventure—"The Eye of Mara," Disneyland, Anaheim, California)

elaborated: "My job and my challenge were to balance the dark side of this *Indiana Jones* saga with as much comedy as I could afford. In many ways, the visual style of the film was conceived when George told me the whole story, which was a very rough sketch of the movie he wanted us to help him construct. I heard a couple of things. I heard Kali Cult and Thuggees. I heard temple of doom, black magic, voodoo, and human sacrifice."

Most people felt that a new Indiana Jones movie, however dark and flawed, is still better than most of the other films out there, and they were right in thinking so. But given the parameters set by Lucas for the story, this film wasn't necessarily doomed—just deeply flawed. In fact, my wife, a huge Indiana Jones fan, who will eagerly sit through repeated viewings of the other movies, refuses to see anything but the beginning and end of this one because of the gross-out factor and (to her) gratuitous darkness.

Stinging from the criticism, George Lucas and Steven Spielberg went back to the model of the first movie when they conceived the third movie, which was fun, entertaining, and a great popcorn movie.

CRITICS' CORNER

Rotten Tomatoes (www.rottentomatoes.com) rating: critics, 91%; fans, 91%.

George Beahm: Well aware that it's necessary to raise the bar with each new film in a series, Lucas deliberately wanted to avoid repeating the elements of the first film, so Lucas made the decision to go dark with this one.

The original title was *Indiana Jones and the Temple of Death,* but that struck everybody as being a bit *too* grim, though that title is consistent with the film. The problem is, how can you effectively merchandise toys and gewgaws to kids whose parents look at the film title and say, "Gee, I don't want my kids walking around Disney World with a T-shirt that says 'death' on it."

So *that* title was killed, and *Temple of Doom* was ultimately chosen. Cheery, no?

What Lucas didn't fully appreciate is that people don't enjoy a movie of such unremitting darkness, even when it comes from crowd-pleaser George Lucas. Viewing such a film is not an escape *from* reality but a reminder *of* it, with the result that many die-hard Indy fans don't put in this DVD as often as, say, the first and third movies.

Moreover, for a movie with licensing aimed at kids, this seemed an inappropriate vehicle. Hardly fare for kids.

Though the movie does have its moments—mostly in the front and back parts—the middle sags uncomfortably and doesn't provide the necessary support the film badly needs.

Roger Ebert (*Chicago Sun-Times*): "This movie is one of the most relentlessly nonstop action pictures ever made, with a virtuoso series of climactic sequences that must last an hour and never stop for a second. It's a roller-coaster ride, a visual extravaganza, a technical triumph, and a whole lot of fun. And it's not simply a retread of *Raiders of the Lost Ark*, the first Indiana Jones movie. It works in a different way, and borrows from different traditions."

Harrison Ford: "This is a completely moral tale and in order to have a moral resolve, evil must be seen to inflict pain. The end of the movie is proof of the viability of goodness. But I do not like films that use violence in a reprehensible way. I do not seek out movies that are bathed in blood."

Willard Huyck (theraider.net): "I would be very conscious in taking a kid to this movie, though. Hopefully, you know your child well enough to know what scares him and what doesn't. But, obviously, if the kid began to get scared, I would leave."

John J. Puccio (dvdtown.com) in a review of the *Complete DVD Movie Collection: The Adventures of Indiana Jones:* "The result was a film that felt more claustrophobic than its predecessor and an adventure that was darker and more somber. In fact, several scenes were considered so grisly, the Motion Picture Association of America's ratings board was inspired to come up with the now-familiar PG-13 classification to supplement their regular PG."

Neil Smith (bbc.co.uk): "Great fun in places, but hardly Indy's finest hour."

Stephen Spielberg: "*Indy II* will not go down in my pantheon as one of my prouder moments."

INDIANA JONES AND THE LAST CRUSADE
Release date: May 14, 1989
Running time: 127 minutes
Box office take (domestic) : $197 million
Soundtrack: John Williams
Oscar win: Best Effects, Sound Effects Editing. (Nominated for Best
Music, Original Score; Best Sound.)
Major cast:
Harrison Ford as *Indiana Jones*
Sean Connery as Indy's father, *Professor Henry Jones*
Denholm Elliott as *Dr. Marcus Brody*
Alison Doody as *Dr. Elsa Schneider*
John Rhys-Davies as *Sallah*
Julian Glover as *Walter Donovan*
River Phoenix as *Young Indiana Jones*
Kevork Malikyan as *Kazim*
Robert Eddison as the *Grail Knight*

SYNOPSIS
In contrast to the previous two movies, which begin with a death-defying scene, this one begins more sedately, though appropriately, by introducing us to Dr. Jones Sr., poring over Grail lore as his son, Indiana, holds the fabled Cross of Coronado, which he rescued from bandits, only to reluctantly relinquish it to the local sheriff, who hands it over to (you guessed it) the bandits.

The past becomes prologue as the movie makes a smooth transition to a scene in which Indy is on board a ship (can you guess its name?) some years later and recovers the Cross of Coronado, showing us his tenacious, persistent side. (He also somehow survives hanging onto a life preserver off the coast of Spain at night—a dubious possibility.)

The Holy Grail cup from the third movie, painted in gold leaf and aged to look like an ancient chalice. (Prop replica by Anthony Magnoli)

As with the first film, we get Nazis galore. We get Hitler (this time, on screen). We get a dogged quest for a religious object in Christian mythology—the Holy Grail cup. The chalice used at the Last Supper, it was also believed to have collected the blood of a crucified Christ from the wound in his side inflicted by the lance of a Roman soldier.

We also get an unexpected but wholly welcome emotional component in the form of Dr. Henry Jones, whose estranged relationship with his son is mended by film's end. Life comes full circle, and father and son finally unite.

With thrills, chills, spills, chase scenes galore, romance, and well-timed humorous scenes, this movie recalls the adventurous fun of the first one and adds a poignant moral dimension, as well.

CRITICS' CORNER

Rotten Tomatoes (www.rottentomatoes.com) rating: critics, 93%; fans, 97%.

George Beahm: The last scene in the movie shows Indy, his father, Sallah, and Dr. Brody riding off into the sunset. George Lucas felt it was the classic scene for such a film and the proper way to end the series, which was originally intended as a trilogy.

Clearly, though, by the third film, Lucas and Spielberg had gotten the Indiana Jones formula honed to perfection. After the missteps in movie #2, movie #3 recaptures the magic, and then some. It was Spielberg's idea to add Indy's search for his father. By fleshing out Indy's early years, by showing us his father, we appreciate Indy's accomplishments even more, knowing he was essentially on his own: his mother gone, his father emotionally distant.

At the end of the movie, when the senior Dr. Jones rescues his son, he doesn't call him "Junior," which is what Indy hates; significantly, the father calls the son by his preferred name, quietly saying, "Indiana, let it go."

Indiana abandons his efforts to grasp the Grail cup and, in a symbolic gesture, reaches out to his father who pulls him back from the precipice. It's a great movie moment and it's one of many reasons why this one resonates with me and remains my eternal favorite.

If the series ended here, Lucas and Spielberg could hang up their fedoras and feel justified that they had accomplished exactly what they set out to do: give the worldwide movie-going audience traditional, big budget, action-adventure movies that harken back to the golden age of Hollywood and pay homage to a kind of moviemaking that had essentially disappeared by the time the first movie came out. As Spielberg explained, *Raiders of the Lost Ark* is "the kind of film my parents used to see Saturday afternoons and which, for some reason, Hollywood stopped producing shortly after my generation was born."

Pete Croatto (Filmcritic.com): "*Indiana Jones and the Last Crusade,* as well as the series' other two outings, is why people go to the movies and keep going back: They want to believe in a world outside of their own. In thirty years, kids will still be arguing over who gets to play Indy and adults will have to fight off the almost unbearable urge to join in the fun. I'll be among them."

Roger Ebert (*Chicago Sun-Times*): "If there is just a shade of disappointment after seeing this movie, it has to be because we will never again have the shock of this material seeming new. *Raiders of the Lost Ark,* now more than ever, seems a turning point in the cinema of escapist entertainment, and there was really no way Spielberg could make it new all over again. What he has done is to take many of the same elements, and apply all of his craft and sense of fun to make them work yet once again. And they do."

Desson Howe (*Washington Post*): "You can safely expect Jones' trademark twisted grin, hat, wisecracks and whip cracks, the pantomime villains, the ingeniously rigged catastrophes . . . and tributes by cine-kid Spielberg to everything from *The Birds* to *She.*"

Caryn James (*New York Times*): "Though it cannot regain the brash originality of *Raiders of the Lost Ark,* in its own way *The Last Crusade* is nearly as good, matching its audience's wildest hopes. Like the two previous films, also directed by Mr. Spielberg, this is one long boisterous adventure, full of storms at sea, exploding boats, and breathless escapes. But Mr. Connery's presence gives resonance to Indiana's life and a slightly slower pace and deeper shading to the film. This is the ultimate quest movie, each discovery leading to a new search—for the father, for the Grail, for faith."

INDIANA JONES AND THE
KINGDOM OF THE CRYSTAL SKULL

Release date: May 22, 2008
Soundtrack: John Williams
Box office take (domestic): estimated up to $400 million
Major cast:
Harrison Ford as *Indiana Jones*
Karen Allen as *Marion Ravenwood*
Ray Winstone as Indy's sidekick, *Mac*
Shia LaBeouf as *Matt Dutton* (rumored to be the son of Indy and Marion)
Cate Blanchett as a Russian interrogator, *Irina Spalko*
John Hurt (rumored to be the late Abner Ravenwood)
Jim Broadbent as an academic colleague

COMMENTS

Languishing in development hell, the fourth Indiana Jones film was a project that seemed as if it would never be made. Finally, a script was produced by Frank Darabont, who had previously worked on scripts for *The Young Indiana Jones Chronicles.*

Indy fans had their hopes buoyed when Darabont turned in the script, and Steven Spielberg loved it; unfortunately, that love was not shared by George Lucas, who shot it down. Darabont told MTV, "It was a tremendous disappointment and a waste of a year. It showed me how badly things can go. I spent a year of very determined effort on something I was very excited about, with a result that [Spielberg and I] felt was terrific. He wanted to direct it as his next movie, and then suddenly the whole thing goes down in flames because George Lucas doesn't like the script."

The challenge of writing a Lucas-proof script then fell to Jeff Nathanson; subsequently, David Koepp worked on it, keeping in mind that fans disliked the dark aspects of *Temple of Doom.*

A half dozen proposed titles were registered with the Motion Pictures Association of America. All were suggestive, leading Indy fans to speculate on the Web as to the film's plot. The titles included *Indiana Jones and the City of Gods; . . . Destroyer of Worlds; . . . Fourth Corner of the Earth; . . . Quest for the Covenant; . . . Lost City of Gold;* and . . . *Kingdom of the Crystal Skull*, which proved to be its final title.

The object at the heart of the fourth film is a Crystal Skull, about which Lucas and company are mum. A Web search, however, turns out numerous references to the legendary powers of crystal skulls, some of which are purported to be alien artifacts.

And Disney fans are well aware that there's an adventure ride at Tokyo Resort called the "Indiana Jones Adventure: Temple of the Crystal Skull." It's a three-minute ride that, according to the official website, allows the rider to "follow in the footsteps of Dr. Indiana Jones in a harrowing life-or-death quest for the legendary Fountain of Youth. But beware—the Fountain is purported to be guarded by a vengeful, supernatural spirit known as the Crystal Skull!"

What, fans wondered, was the Crystal Skull in this movie?

Mindful of the nineteen-year time lapse between the last Indiana Jones film and the current one, Spielberg and Lucas wisely chose not to cover familiar territory by setting it in the 1940s. Instead, the storyline updates Indy to the 1950s, at the height of the Cold War between the United States and its nemesis, the USSR.

The film also brings back the most popular Indiana Jones heroine—the spunky Marion Ravenwood, brilliantly played by Karen Allen. And because the studio is ever mindful of the need to connect with the film's principal audience (young adults and teenagers), Indy newcomer Shia LaBeouf joins the cast, with the rumor that he's the love child of Indy and Marion, which strikes me as plausible. (We don't know, after all, what happened to Marion after the first film, but surely she and Indy kept in touch over the years, right?)

Because of the long interval since the last Indy movie, promotion began in earnest well before the film's release. There was a welcome repackaging of the *Young Indiana Jones Chronicles,* an official website (www.indiana jones.com), tantalizing snippets of news and photos that appeared on the Web, and a closed circuit, live appearance of Harrison Ford and Steven Spielberg on the shooting set. This appearance was broadcast to the comic-book crowd at the massively attended San Diego Comicon (the holy Mecca for geeks worldwide), and an impressive line-up of licensees brought out framable photos, trading cards, toys, clothing, computer games, apparel, books, and high-end collectibles (sculptures, busts, and replica props).

The film industry depends on what they call "tentpole" movies—films with substantial box office receipts, sufficient to prop up flagging ticket sales for the off-season. There's no question that *Indiana Jones and the Kingdom of the Crystal Skull* will be a box office smash, a "tentpole" summer film. The only question is: *how* big? Estimates range up to $400 million in the U.S. alone.

Likely to rejuvenate the franchise, the fourth film may well be Indy's last outing. Harrison Ford (as of July 2008) will be sixty-six years old—old enough to draw retirement from his fictional Marshall College, where he held (mostly) dewy-eyed coeds in thrall as he told them about the secrets, the mysteries, and the wonders of past civilizations, lost worlds, and the artifacts discovered, including (presumably) crystal skulls.

A WORD FROM THE TOP

NOTE: The following quotes are from *Vanity Fair* (Feb 2008) and the *Vanity Fair* official website.

Harrison Ford (on his character and costume): "It's a very bizarre costume, when you think about it. It's this guy sporting a whip, who's off usually for someplace really hot in his leather jacket. There's something about the character that I guess is a good fit for me, because the minute I put the costume on, I recognize the tone that we need, and I feel confident and clear about the character."

George Lucas (on the Indiana Jones character): "Indiana Jones gets in over his head and he can't handle it. It's only by sheer, last-second skill, or luck, or whatever, that he actually gets himself out of it. You can't create a character like that without knowing that someone like Harrison can have the right, befuddled, oh-my-God-I'm-gonna-die look. And you're right there with him. He's Everyman. He's us."

Steven Spielberg (on the Indiana Jones character): "I mean, Indiana Jones is not a perfect hero, and his imperfections, I think, make the audience feel that, with a little more exercise and a little more courage, they could be just like him. So he's not the Terminator. He's not so far away from the people who go to see the movies that he's inaccessible to their own dreams and aspirations."

Official Pix is *the* source for official Indiana Jones photographs. At a time when forged signatures and cheap knock-off prints are offered on eBay by unscrupulous dealers looking to line their pockets with ill-gotten gains, it's comforting to know that there's one place where Indy fans can get licensed photographs at an affordable price from a trusted manufacturer.

Official Pix had its start in 2001, when it began selling *Star Wars* autographs in a marketplace rife with counterfeited prints. Since then, Official Pix has worked with more than one hundred celebrities in the *Star Wars* universe, including the films' principal and supporting actors.

In 2007, in time for the fourth Indy film, Official Pix announced a line of high-quality photographs, each bearing the company's holographic label to verify its authenticity. Selling through its own website and through the official *Star Wars* online store, Official Pix debuted its Indiana Jones line of full color prints (8 x 10 inches on Fuji photographic paper) that retail for $5.99 in open editions.

The first licensed photo in the Indy line (see above) was taken by Steven Spielberg. Showing Harrison Ford taking a break from the shooting, the 11 x 14–inch photo, limited to 250 numbered copies, sold out immediately upon publication. Although more photos from *Indiana Jones and the Kingdom of the Crystal Skull* are forthcoming, this candid snapshot will remain my personal favorite because it captures an unstaged moment: world-weary but wiser for the passage of time, Harrison Ford as Indy affirms the adage that it's not the years but the mileage.

The company can be reached at: Official Pix (www.officialpix.com), PO Box 292066, Lewisville, TX 75029. E-mail: info@officialpix.com. Phone: (972) 420-8639. Fax: (972) 692-5144.

A WALK THROUGH THE TWENTIETH CENTURY: HISTORY WITH INDIANA JONES, OR *THE YOUNG INDIANA JONES CHRONICLES*

"It started out of a love of an idea. I have an educational foundation working with interactive projects, and I got this idea to get kids involved in history through the Young Indiana Jones character," said Lucas about the inspiration that led to the creation of the series. "The turn of the century is my favorite part of history because it has so much to do with the emergence of the modern age we live in today. It seemed like such a great idea and such an interesting adventure that I just got lured into it by the creative potential. I took it to the network and said, 'Would

Indiana Jones's diary, containing his life story from 1908 to 1951. (Prop replica by Anthony Magnoli)

you be interested in this? It's a little bit esoteric for television,' but they said, 'Great!' They've been very cooperative and we've been off making this adventure ever since . . . and it has been a true adventure."

As any film director will tell you, trying to tell a long story and compress it for the silver screen is a matter of endless frustration and compromise, which is why some turn to television, which allows for the luxury of time. Instead of having a life's story compressed into two hours, with the aggravation of flashbacks, a television series allows the story to unfold at a pace that serves it best.

For George Lucas, the Indiana Jones movies showed three specific episodes of the adventuring archaeologist, but gave no real sense of his life. What was Indy like as a child? What events shaped him? What was Indy like as a young adult? What major events into the tumultuous twentieth century shaped his worldview? Clearly, this was far more than could ever be adequately covered on the silver screen. The workable alternative was to come up with a series for television. In this fashion, the whole story of Indy Jones, from youth to adult, could be told. Moreover, it would be an opportunity to take a walk, as it were, through the twentieth century by having Indy meet, and be inspired by, leading figures in history.

As Lucas explained, "The show explores how Indiana Jones got to be the way he is. How, like in the features, did he learn to speak so many languages? Where did he pick that up? How did he decide to become an archaeologist? There are so many fascinating things about the character that you can't deal with in the features because they move along so fast on an action level."

Each episode was forty-five minutes (with commercials, one hour); thirty-six episodes aired. The series ran on ABC TV for three seasons, from 1992 to 1994, with a final episode that aired in June 1996. It then went to the Family Channel, where even fewer saw it. Subsequently reedited, the episodes were intended to be released for home video, but only twelve of the intended twenty-two were actually released, because of disappointing sales.

Clearly, fans were willing to queue up for the movies, but the home video market for this series never caught fire with the viewing public, principally because some of the stories lacked what viewers had come to expect of any project to which the Indiana Jones name was attached: the same kind of relentless pacing that characterizes the movies. As Lucas explained to the *Los Angeles Times* in 2007, "It didn't matter how many times I said it was a coming-of-age series about a young boy's exploration of history, people still expected to see that rolling boulder."

Waiting in line can be dangerous. Be careful where you put your hat!
(Indiana Jones Adventure—"The Eye of Mara," Disneyland, Anaheim, California)

With the demise of the episodes on VHS tape, bootleg editions of all the episodes were subsequently released on DVD, with (predictably) poor quality audio and video. Fans deserved better, and the bootlegs seemed to me to be a sad endnote to what was a worthwhile, educational series.

But time changes everything and the young Indiana Jones is back, this time in a new and improved version. Carefully and lovingly restored to enhance the sound and picture quality, the episodes were released in three collections in October 2007, December 2007, and April 2008.

Rather than material simply cobbled together for a quick buck, the packages are works of art. "Over the past four years," reported Geoff Boucher for the *Los Angeles Times,* "Lucas and Paramount Home Video have pumped millions of dollars into reframing *Young Indiana* as a lavish, three-volume library of DVDs with a staggering number of extras, including ninety-four highly polished documentaries on famous people and moments in history. That grand content and the packaging and marketing commitment to the project are the sort you might expect for an anniversary reissue of *Gone with the Wind,* not a show that was dropped by ABC after two seasons and moved on to the smaller stage of the Family Channel."

At $129.99 per set, the original footage has been meticulously restored (as is Lucas's custom when reissuing material); additionally, there are dozens of documentaries, a historical overview, an interactive game, and a timeline. Of this supplementary material, the documentaries are especially promising, since there is commentary from leading contemporary figures, including General Colin Powell, Henry Kissinger, Gloria Steinem, Martin Scorsese, Barbara Boxer, James Earl Jones, Hal David, Deepak Chopra, and professors from leading universities.

Not surprisingly, the episodes themselves vary in quality, ranging from fair-to-middling to excellent, as one of its scriptwriters, Frank Darabont, observed. Overall, though, there's a lot of storytelling here, with the added bonus of learning as much as you'd wish about twentieth-century history. (For those who want their dollops of history extracted from the stories, the documentaries are uniformly excellent.)

Let's overlook the obvious fact that there's no way *anyone* could have met, as young Indy does, so many prominent figures of the twentieth century, no matter how well traveled. But in this case, the stories serve the goal of hooking kids on history by making it come alive: First, get their attention and then tell and show them what you really want them to know.

With the complete canon of *The Young Indiana Jones Chronicles* now available, what's on each disc? Glad you asked. (I've seen a sampling of the episodes from Volume One and can affirm that the official write-ups are mostly accurate, with just a hint of occasional hyperbole.)

The Adventures of Young Indiana Jones: Volume One

DISC 1: "MY FIRST ADVENTURE"

Historical figure: T. E. Lawrence, better known as Lawrence of Arabia.

Locations: Valley of the Kings in Egypt; North Africa; child slave markets of Marrakech.

Plot: Indy, on an archaeological dig, finds more than he bargains for when he uncovers a mummy, a recent corpse, and a murder mystery. A young Indy solves the murder with the help of T. E. Lawrence.

Documentaries:
Archaeology: Unearthing Our Past
Howard Carter and the Tomb of Tutankhamen
Colonel Lawrence's War: T. E. Lawrence and Arabia
From Slavery to Freedom

DISC 2: "PASSION FOR LIFE"

Historical figures: Teddy Roosevelt; artists Pablo Picasso, Edgar Degas, and Norman Rockwell.

Locations: Masai Mara game reserve in Kenya; Paris.

Plot: Indy is on a safari with Teddy Roosevelt but becomes lost and must fend for himself. Indy later joins a young Norman Rockwell in Paris as they enjoy the city's turbulent nightlife that swirls around Picasso.

Documentaries:
Theodore Roosevelt and the American Century
Ecology: Pulse of the Planet
American Dreams: Norman Rockwell and the *Saturday Evening Post*
Art Rebellion: The Making of the Modern
Edgar Degas: Reluctant Rebel
Braque + Picasso: A Collaboration Cubed

As seen in the first Indiana Jones film, this is a model of the WWI
tank used in the chase scene. (Designed by Disney Imagineer Tim Kirk)

DISC 3: "THE PERILS OF CUPID"

Historical figures: the Archduke Franz Ferdinand of Austria; psychol-
ogists Sigmund Freud and Carl Jung; opera composer Giacomo
Puccini.

Locations: Vienna, Austria; Florence, Italy.

Plot: Indy falls in love with the daughter of the Archduke Franz
Ferdinand of Austria, who will soon be assassinated in Sarajevo.
Young at heart but clearly out of his element, Indy solicits advice
from Freud and Jung. . . . On another romantic front, Indy finds
himself trying to reunite his parents before his mother succumbs
to the undeniable charms of Puccini.

Documentaries:
Giacomo Puccini, "Music of the Heart"
It's Opera!

The Archduke's Last Journey: End of an Era
Powder Keg: Europe 1900 to 1914
Sigmund Freud: Exploring the Unconscious
Carl Jung and the Journey of Self-Discovery
Psychology: Charting the Human Mind

DISC 4: "TRAVELS WITH FATHER"

Historical figure: Russian novelist Leo Tolstoy.

Locations: Russia; a Greek monastery.

Plot: After running away from home, Indy finds himself in Russia, where he sees its beauty . . . and ugliness, from the elegant palaces to the hardscrabble lives of the peasants. Indy, traveling with Tolstoy, meets gypsies and Cossacks. In the end, Indy realizes the old truth that home is where the heart is, as he rejoins his parents at a mountaintop monastery in Greece.

A truck with "found" artifacts evoking the marketplace scene
in the first Indiana Jones movie; a static display. (Indiana
Jones Stunt Spectacular, Walt Disney World, Orlando, Florida)

Documentaries:
    Seeking Truth: The Life of Leo Tolstoy
    Unquiet Voices: Russian Writers and the State
    Aristotle: Creating Foundations
    Ancient Questions: Philosophy and Our Search for Meaning

DISC 5: "JOURNEY OF RADIANCE"

Historical figure: the leader of the Theosophy movement, Jiddu Krishnamurti.

Location: in the Far East, the Holy City of Benares.

Plot: Indy becomes friends with Krishnamurti, who shows him the enduring power of faith. Later, Indy, traveling with his mother, is stricken with typhoid fever but is saved by Chinese villagers who use "traditional medical techniques" to save his life.

Documentaries:
    Jiddu Krishnamurti: The Reluctant Messiah
    Annie Besant: An Unlikely Rebel
    Medicine in the Middle Kingdom
    Eastern Spirituality: The Road to Enlightenment

DISC 6: "SPRING BREAK ADVENTURE"

Historical figures: inventor Thomas Edison, Mexican revolutionary Pancho Villa, U.S. Army officer General George S. Patton.

Location: American Southwest.

Plot: Indy and his main squeeze, Nancy Stratemeyer, visit Edison's lab. He finds himself embroiled in a German plot to steal Edison's top-secret project. Indy's family, concerned for his safety, send him off to New Mexico to visit his aunt. But it proves to be no sanctuary when Pancho Villa kidnaps him and Indy finds himself in the middle of the Mexican Revolution. Indy also meets, in a barroom, a young George Patton.

Documentaries:
Thomas Alva Edison: Lighting Up the World
Invention and Innovation: What's Behind a Good Idea?
The Mystery of Edward Stratemeyer (creator of the Nancy Drew mystery book series)
Wanted: Dead or Alive: Pancho Villa and the American Invasion of Mexico
General John J. Pershing and His American Army
General George S. Patton: American Achilles

DISC 7: "LOVE'S SWEET SONG"

Historical figure: Winston Churchill.

Locations: Ireland and England.

Plot: In Ireland, Indy falls for a young girl whose brother is a member of the Irish resistance movement. In England, Indy falls for a young woman who is involved in the women's rights movement.

Documentaries:
Easter Rising: The Poets' Rebellion
The Passions of William Butler Yeats
Sean O'Casey vs. Ireland
Ireland: The Power of the Poets
Winston Churchill: The Lion's Roar
Demanding the Vote: The Pankhursts and British Fighting for the Vote: Women's Suffrage in America

Special Features Interactive Disc:
This disc provides an interactive timeline showing the history and locations of Indy's adventures, a historical feature: The Promise of Progress, and an interactive game involving the Industrial Revolution.

The bad guys lose their footing and go for a "ride." (Indiana Jones Stunt Spectacular, Walt Disney World, Orlando, Florida)

The Adventures of Young Indiana Jones: Volume Two

DISC 8: "THE TRENCHES OF HELL"

Historical figure: French leader Charles de Gaulle.

Location: Europe.

Plot: Indy, an enlistee in the Belgian Army, fights in the Battle of Somme. He is captured, along with de Gaulle, by the Germans. Both are put in a POW camp and soon hatch a plan to escape.

Documentaries:
Siegfried Sassoon: "A War Poet's Journey"
Robert Graves and the White Goddess
I Am France: The Myth of Charles de Gaulle
The Somme: A Storm of Steel

DISC 9: "DEMONS OF DECEPTION"

Historical figure: female spy Mata Hari.

Location: Paris.

Plot: Indy realizes that his superior officers are more interested in the mission than in the men, regardless of the human costs. He takes refuge in the arms of Mata Hari in Paris, but finds no solace as she lives up to her billing.

Documentaries:
Marshal Petain's Fall from Grace
Flirting with Danger: The Fantasy of Mata Hari
Into the Furnace: The Battle of Verdun
Reading the Enemy's Mind: Espionage in World War I

A Nazi on a vintage motorcycle comes to the aid of his fellow soldiers.
(Indiana Jones Stunt Spectacular, Walt Disney World, Orlando, Florida)

DISC 10: "PHANTOM TRAIN OF DOOM"

Historical figures: Margaret Trappe, first female "great white hunter" in Africa; German officer Colonel Paul Emil von Lettow-Vorbeck; South African statesman and soldier (and former British citizen) General Jan Christiaan Smuts; British Intelligence officer Colonel Richard Meinertzhagen; British explorer and hunter Frederick Selous.

Location: Africa.

Plot: Indy is assigned the mission of destroying a large German howitzer hidden inside a mountain.

Documentaries:
Chasing the Phantom: Paul von Lettow-Vorbeck
Dreaming of Africa: The Life of Frederick Selous
At Home and Abroad: The Two Faces of Jan Smuts

DISC 11: "OGANGA, THE GIVER AND TAKER OF LIFE"

Historical figure: Dr. Albert Schweitzer.

Location: Africa.

Plot: Indy saves a child while on a military mission. Working his way across Africa, Indy becomes increasingly depressed as he witnesses the desperate living conditions of Africans. But he's inspired by the sterling example of Dr. Albert Schweitzer at his jungle hospital.

Documentaries:
Albert Schweitzer: Reverence for Life
Waging Peace: The Rise of Pacifism
Congo: A Curse of Riches

DISC 12: "ATTACK OF THE HAWKMEN"

Historical figures: German flying ace, the Red Baron (Manfred von Richthofen); German aircraft designer Anthony Fokker.

Location: Germany.

Plot: Flying on reconnaissance missions over Germany with the French unit, the Lafayette Escadrille, Indy and the Red Baron battle it out in an aerial dogfight. Working undercover, Indy uncovers a secret German weapon that promises to change the course of the war. Indy must then alert the Allies of its presence or destroy it.

Documentaries:
Blood Red: The Life and Death of Manfred von Richthofen
Anthony Fokker: The Flying Dutchman
Flying High for France: The Lafayette Escadrille
War in the Third Dimension: Aerial Warfare in World War I

DISC 13: "ADVENTURES IN THE SECRET SERVICE"

Historical figure: Emperor Karl of Austria.

Locations: German-occupied territories in Europe; Russia.

Plot: Hoping to end the war, Indy goes on a diplomatic mission to see Emperor Karl of Austria. Indy also finds himself in Russia during the Bolshevik Revolution.

Documentaries:
Karl: The Last Hapsburg Emperor
V. I. Lenin: History Will Not Forgive Us
The Russian Revolution: All Power to the Soviets!

DISC 14: "ESPIONAGE ESCAPADES"

Historical figures: artist Pablo Picasso and novelist Franz Kafka.

Locations: Spain; Prague, Czechoslovakia.

Plot: Indy attempts to discredit German diplomats as he goes undercover as a dancer for the famous Ballets Russes, where he meets (again) Picasso.

Documentaries:
Impresario: Sergei Diaghilev and the Ballets Russes

Franz Kafka's Dark Truth
Ballet: The Art of Dance

DISC 15: "DAREDEVILS OF THE DESERT"

Historical figures: Australian Lighthorsemen Regiment

Locations: Beersheba, Middle East.

Plot: Indy works with a beautiful belly dancer who assists him in an effort to prevent a bomb from detonating in a city's water supply.

Documentaries:
Col. Lawrence's War: T. E. Lawrence and Arabia
Lines in the Sand: The Middle East and the Great War

Indy and Marion employ a rope escape in the marketplace scene recreated from the first movie. (Indiana Jones Stunt Spectacular, Walt Disney World, Orlando, Florida)

The Adventures of Young Indiana Jones: Volume Three

DISC 16: "TALES OF INNOCENCE"

Historical figures: writers Ernest Hemingway and Edith Wharton.

Locations: Italy; North Africa.

Plot: Indy is behind enemy lines on a propaganda assignment. He also is in competition with Ernest Hemingway over an Italian girl. Wounded in action, Indy is transferred to North Africa. He joins the French Foreign Legion, infested with a traitor in its ranks. Indy flirts with Edith Wharton.

Documentaries:
Unhealed Wounds: The Life of Ernest Hemingway
The Secret Life of Edith Wharton
Lowell Thomas: American Storyteller
The French Foreign Legion: The World's Most Legendary
    Fighting Force

DISC 17: "MASKS OF EVIL"

Historical figure: Vlad the Impaler.

Locations: Istanbul; Transylvania.

Plot: In Istanbul, Indy uncovers a plot to assassinate French espionage agents. In Transylvania, Indy fights Vlad the Impaler and his army of the living dead.

Documentaries:
For the People, Despite the People: The Ataturk Revolution
The Greedy Heart of Halide Edib
Dracula: Fact and Fiction
The Ottoman Empire: A World of Difference

At the entrance to Adventureland, a colorful wood carving exhibits disrespect to passersby. (Magic Kingdom, Walt Disney World, Orlando, Florida)

DISC 18: "TREASURE OF THE PEACOCK'S EYE"

Historical figure: anthropologist Bronislaw Malinowski.

Locations: London; Alexandria; South China Sea.

Plot: After the war's end, Indy is searching for a diamond that makes its way from London to the Middle East and finally the South China Sea, where Indy battles with Chinese pirates and is later captured by headhunters, only to be rescued by Malinowski.

Documentaries:
    Bronislaw Malinowski: God Professor
    Anthropology: Looking at the Human Condition
    New Guinea: Paradise in Peril

DISC 19: "WINDS OF CHANGE"

Historical figures: T. E. Lawrence, Prince Faisal of Arabia, Ho Chi Minh, Paul Robeson.

Locations: Paris; United States.

Plot: Indy, a translator in Paris, is disillusioned by the brutality of realpolitik. When he heads home, he sees the ugly face of bigotry as experienced by a childhood friend, Paul Robeson, noted for his early advocacy of civil rights.

Documentaries:
    Woodrow Wilson: American Idealist
    Gertrude Bell: Iraq's Uncrowned Queen
    Ho Chi Minh: The Price of Freedom
    Paul Robeson: Scandalize My Name
    Robert Goddard: Mr. Rocket Science
    The Best Intentions: The Paris Peace Conference and the Treaty
        of Versailles

DISC 20: "THE MYSTERY OF THE BLUES"

Historical figures: jazz great Sidney Bechet, Chicago thug Al Capone, and Untouchable Eliot Ness.

Location: Chicago.

Plot: Indy is a college student with a growing interest in jazz. He meets jazz great Sidney Bechet, who encourages his fledgling interest. Working together, Indy and his college roomie Eliot Ness foil Al Capone's men and solve a murder.
Note: This is the only episode in which Harrison Ford appears,

bookending the story. We discover how Ford's interest in all that jazz helps him out of a tough spot.

Documentaries:
Al "Scarface" Capone: The Original Gangster
Ben Hecht: Shakespeare of Hollywood
On the Trail of Eliot Ness
Louis Armstrong: Ambassador of Jazz
Jazz: Rhythms of Freedom
Prohibition: America on the Rocks
Hellfighters: Harlem's Heroes of World War I

Indy and Marion escape from a burning WWI airplane. (Indiana Jones Stunt Spectacular, Walt Disney World, Orlando, Florida)

DISC 21: "THE SCANDAL OF 1920"

Historical figures: composer George Gershwin, members of the Algonquin Round Table.

Location: New York City.

Plot: Indy has his hands full, on and off stage. Dating three different women, working with Gershwin to stage-manage a Broadway play, partying with New York high society, reading poetry with bohemians in Greenwich Village, and matching wits with members of the Algonquin Round Table, Indy takes a juicy bite out of the Big Apple.

Documentaries:
Tin Pan Alley: Soundtrack of America
Broadway: America Center Stage
Wonderful Nonsense: The Algonquin Round Table

DISC 22: "THE HOLLYWOOD FOLLIES"

Historical figures: directors Erich von Stroheim and John Ford, Wyatt Earp.

Location: Hollywood.

Plot: After locking horns with film director Eric von Stroheim, Indy is disenchanted with the film industry. But all that is put behind him when director John Ford—aided by aging gunman Wyatt Earp—helps him rediscover its magic.

Documentaries:
    Erich von Stroheim: The Profligate Genius
    The World of John Ford
    Irving Thalberg: Hollywood's Boy Wonder
    The Rise of the Moguls: The Men Who Built Hollywood

They roll, tumble, and fall, but are they acrobats or something else? Those villagers better watch out. (Indiana Jones Stunt Spectacular, Walt Disney World, Orlando, Florida)

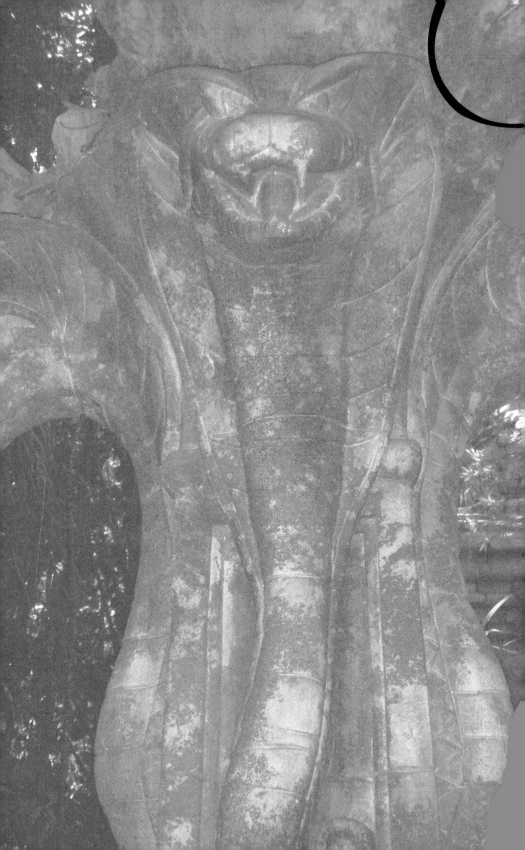

PART 2

Indiana Jones: Fact, Fiction, or Folklore?

"ONE OF THE GREAT DANGERS IN ARCHAEOLOGY . . .

NOT THE LIFE AND LIMB, ALTHOUGH THAT DOES SOME-

TIMES TAKE PLACE. . . . I'M TALKING ABOUT FOLKLORE."

—Indiana Jones, *Raiders of the Lost Ark*

In the first and third Indiana Jones movies, we see Dr. Jones in an academic setting. He's teaching class, which is what you'd expect from a professor of archaeology. That part rings true, but obviously the audience is not going to sit for two hours listening to Dr. Jones merely talk about ancient artifacts, nor would they be entranced by long sequences showing Indy at a dig in Egypt, carefully digging and sifting through sand, excavating pieces of pottery, for eventual study.

Let's face it, Indy is much more adventurer than archaeologist, and we wouldn't have it any other way. Frankly, we go to the movies not necessarily to learn about our world but to be entertained and distracted from our mundane lives.

Hollywood, of course, takes liberal license in movies and bends the truth, reshapes history, and outright invents things as convenient, so what you see on the screen should not be taken as gospel. In short, don't expect Hollywood to be historically accurate.

Unfortunately, because most people's knowledge of history is woefully inadequate, and because there are pockets of gullible people who will believe anything no matter how outlandish, movies that take liberal license for entertainment purposes are sometimes taken as accurate. And people take what they see far too seriously.

It's good to keep in mind what George Lucas said after hearing about the extent to which *Star Wars* fans were consumed by their interest in his pop-cult, Joseph Campbell–inspired space fantasy: "It's just a movie."

Likewise, it's good to remember that the Indiana Jones movies are artful blends of fact and fantasy, reality and the supernatural. In other words, sometimes the story pays homage to history, but more often, history is liberally and imaginatively *reinterpreted* to serve the story.

The section that follows talks about some of the series' colorful discrepancies and separates fact from fiction.

RAIDERS OF THE LOST ARK:
SOUTH AMERICA AND EGYPT, 1936

Do tribesmen in South America use poison darts?

In a word, yes. In its entry on poison dart frogs, Sheppard Software (www.sheppardsoftware.com) affirms that the poison used is from the poison dart frogs that are indigenous to Central America and South America. More specifically, it says, the Noanama Choco and Embera Choco Indians of western Colombia harvest the highly poisonous toxins of the frogs with which to tip their darts (not arrows).

Because the frogs' neurotoxin is fast acting and fatal, especially through mucous membranes (like the human tongue), it's not likely that Satipo (who, at the beginning of the first film, accompanies but soon betrays Indiana Jones, and gets shafted as a result) would have *tasted* the tip of the poison dart to check its freshness. The simple truth is that Satipo would have died in minutes, and painfully, too.

Important safety tip: Do *not* taste the poison to determine its freshness, for you may find it will disagree with you.

Which South American tribe speaks Hovitos?

None.

Too bad for Indiana Jones, who manages to disarm a shady travel guide, trigger booby traps without harming himself, walk a labyrinthine path to avoid setting off more booby traps, replace a golden idol with a bagful of sand, slip under a stone barrier threatening to isolate him in the booby-trapped corridor, and run like hell carrying the idol despite a barrage of arrows shooting from the mouths of stone figurines from both flanks of the corridor, only to be nearly flattened by a two-ton boulder. (Makes you think twice about being an adventurer-archaeologist, doesn't it?)

In other words, Indy knows he's going into a dangerous part of the world, and he didn't bring a guidebook or English-to-Hovitos dictionary? (In later films, Indy speaks other languages fluently, so perhaps he wised up and decided to learn the local tongue *before* arriving on the scene.)

Since Indy's arch nemesis, a French archaeologist named Dr. Rene Belloq, speaks Hovitos fluently, it's clear that it's far from being a dead language.

Important travel tip: Bone up on the native tongue before heading off to strange places where you might run into unfriendly locals or grasping archaeologists who want you to do the dirty work and then take whatever you find out of your hands.

What are the chances that Indiana Jones would correctly guesstimate the proper amount of sand to be put in a bag to replace the weight of a golden statue so that it would not set off any booby traps?

Not very good, unless he knew a lot about physics and metallurgy, had a way to calculate measurements quickly and accurately, and had Lady Luck on his side.

After cleverly negotiating a series of daunting booby traps, Indy is standing in front of the Golden Idol of Fertility, which he must replace with a bag of sand of *exactly* the same weight to avoid triggering any booby traps. Lacking any measuring or computational tools, he merely eyeballs it. He hefts the bag and pulls out a handful, to let it run through his fingers, only to discard it. Then he carefully tips over the statue but replaces it immediately with the bag of sand . . . hoping not to set off its booby trap. And fails. So he runs for dear life.

Let's do the *rough* math, keeping in mind sand and gold have different specific gravities. And remember that I'm simply trying to establish that it'd take a *lot* bigger bag of sand than what Indy had in order to exchange it pound for pound with the statue, and not be exact to the point of nerd-dom.

Loose sand has a weight of 100 pounds per cubic foot. Pure 24 karat gold, however, has a weight of 1,204 pounds per cubic foot; therefore, gold is a little more than twelve times the weight of the same volume of sand.

As the statue measures 5.91 x 5.91 x 7.87 inches (or 15 x 15 x 20 centimeters), it is approximately 275 cubic inches. Since a cubic foot is 1,728 inches and the statue is one-sixteenth its size, the statue weighs roughly 75 pounds, about the weight of a small child. The bag of sand, then, would have to be about three-quarters the size of a cubic foot, which it clearly isn't. So Indy was a bit off in his math! No wonder he triggered the booby trap!

Of course, those wily Indians may have booby-trapped it so that no matter what was exchanged weight-wise, the trap would go off. In any case, Indy did escape with the Golden Idol of Fertility, only to have the nefarious Dr. Belloq misappropriate it. Or, as Belloq puts it, "Dr. Jones, there's nothing you can possess that I cannot take away."

Important survival tip: Pack a slide rule (the computational "computer" of its time).

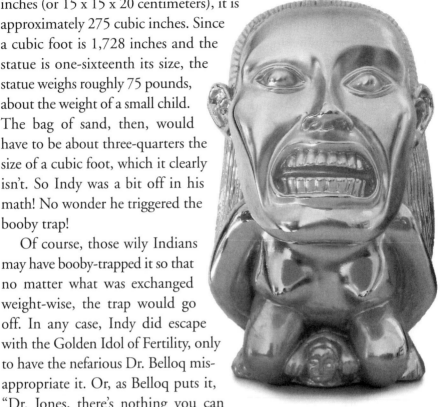

This Golden Idol of Fertility weighs nearly twelve pounds. It was constructed using the lost-wax method of casting and plated in 24k gold. (Prop replica by Anthony Magnoli)

How easy is it to learn how to use a bullwhip effectively?

Harder than you think.

You may recall that, in the third film, we see a young Indy Jones who, when he finds himself in a corner with a lion preparing to attack, grabs a bullwhip and inexpertly cracks it, cutting himself on his chin.

According to David Morgan (www.davidmorgan.com), "We supplied over 30 bullwhips of the 450 series for the Indiana Jones movies. These ranged in length from 6 feet to 16 feet. The standard length carried in the movies was the No. 455 10-foot Bullwhip. The other lengths were used in special stunts. All were in the natural tan color. In addition to our whips, a child's whip made by Swayne, Adney, and Briggs was used in a scene from Indiana Jones' youth *[Lost Crusade]*."

The No. 455 Bullwhip, says Morgan, "became an icon when it was so skillfully woven into the story by Glenn Randall, the stunt director for the first movie. It became a recognized part of the Indiana Jones character, and an ongoing factor in maintaining the suspense of the story. Equally as important, the association of this whip with these outstanding movies led to a resurgence in interest in whips in movies, stage performances, and in sports whip-cracking. There are now large numbers of Indiana Jones fans, many cracking whips."

For those interested in serious whip-cracking, the ten-foot bullwhip (stock number 455) by David Morgan is your first choice, but it'll set you back $840.

As you may expect, Morgan takes his whip-cracking *very* seriously and cautions, "Remember, the tip of a whip moves fast, with the speed and energy to break the sound barrier. It can damage people and objects. Handle your whip safely, in a clear area."

He recommends buying a high-quality whip, noting that it will "move out and crack when it is thrown with very little effort, and will retain its shape and structural integrity over many years of use."

As for learning how to crack a whip, you may have to learn on your own, but there are several good videos that show and tell. John Brady, a celebrated Australian whip artist, sells a $20 video (available from www.davidmorgan.com). Brady is considered "an outstanding artist with a unique range of whip routines. He has developed and polished routines of great diversity during long years of experience in country shows in Australia and Wild West and stage shows in the U.S."

Now, are you ready to learn? Well, *get cracking!*

Indiana Jones has a fear of snakes. Is this a rational fear? How common is it?

Called ophidiophobia, fear of snakes is fairly common.

There are numerous reasons why people fear snakes, but in Indy's case, an early childhood experience shook him up: In *The Lost Crusade*, as a teenager trying to escape treasure hunters who are chasing him as he

The head of a stone serpent peers over the milling crowd lined up to take the ride of their lives. (Indiana Jones Adventure— "The Eye of Mara," Disneyland, Anaheim, California)

jumps from railcar to railcar on a moving circus train, he falls through the roof of a railcar containing thousands of snakes. He's understandably spooked and, years later, in *Raiders of the Lost Ark,* he narrowly escapes death by outrunning a tribe of South American Indians armed with poison dart guns and bows and arrows only to find himself in the front cockpit of a seaplane that, to his horror, he's sharing with a large snake named Reggie that belongs to the pilot. On seeing the snake, Indy yells, "There's a big snake in the plane! I hate snakes! I hate 'em!"

The pilot nonchalantly replies, "Come on, show a little backbone."

Later in *Raiders,* Indy has located the cavernous vault containing the treasured lost Ark of the Covenant, reputed to hold the broken pieces of the Ten Commandments. Indy asks his Egyptian friend Sallah, "Why is the floor moving?" It's moving because, as Indy finds out, it's writhing with snakes. Thousands of them. Asps, too. *Very* dangerous.

Snake phobia is common but can be cured, according to the folks at www.phobia-fear-release.com. But in the meantime, people like Indy who suffer from ophidiophobia can expect to suffer a wide range of symptoms:

breathlessness, dizziness, excessive sweating, nausea, dry mouth, feeling sick, shaking, heart palpitations, inability to speak or think clearly, a sensation of detachment from reality, or a full-blown anxiety attack.

So there's Indy, flying over a South American rain forest, sharing his personal space with a large snake of indeterminate origin (but likely not venomous), and almost certainly suffering through all the symptoms I've listed.

Come on, Dr. Jones, don't be a girly man!

Is there such a thing as an International Treaty for the Protection of Antiquities?

There is, but not in those exact words, and not until well after the 1930s setting of the early Indy movies.

In fact, it wasn't until 1954 that this critical matter was adequately addressed in an international forum, resulting in the Convention for the Protection of Cultural Property in the Event of Armed Conflict. As explained on the UNESCO (United Nations Educational, Scientific and Cultural Organization) website (http://portal.unesco.org), it was adopted "in the wake of massive destruction of the cultural heritage in the Second World War" and "covers immovables and movables, including monuments of architecture, art or history, archaeological sites, works of art, manuscripts, books and other objects of artistic, historical or archaeolog-

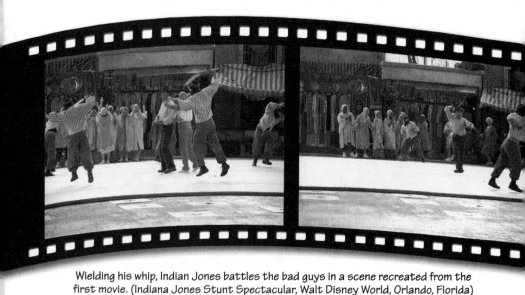

Wielding his whip, Indian Jones battles the bad guys in a scene recreated from the first movie. (Indiana Jones Stunt Spectacular, Walt Disney World, Orlando, Florida)

ical interest, as well as scientific collections of all kinds regardless of their origin or ownership."

Keeping in mind the timeframe of the first three Indiana Jones movies (1936, 1935, and 1938), The Hague Convention of 1954 is the closest thing to what Dr. Marcus Brody had cited, though obviously some years later.

Did the Nazis have a dig near Cairo for a lost city named Tanis where they expected to find the Lost Ark of the Covenant?

There was never a Nazi dig named the "Tanis Development" at that city, which we are told in the Indiana Jones movie is a lost city that was purportedly destroyed in a sandstorm, where it lay buried until 1936 when the Nazis discovered it.

Tanis, a well-known site among Egyptologists, is located in the Northeast Delta of Egypt. Located east of Alexandria and north of Cairo, Tanis was first excavated in 1860, but it wasn't until 1939 that a subsequent dig struck pay dirt. Though valuables had been plundered during the early digs, French Egyptologist Pierre Montet discovered archaeological treasures galore, most notably sarcophagi. The ruins of several major temples housed Osorkon II, Pami, Psusennes I, Amenemope, and Shoshenq III, among others. The site included golden treasures as well: bracelets, pectorals, and funerary masks, to name some of the most prominent finds.

Tanis wasn't, however, the real resting place for the fabled lost Ark of the Covenant. For that, the Nazis would have had to look elsewhere. . . . As Indy and his friend Sallah observed, "They are digging in the wrong place!"

As for Hitler's interest in the Lost Ark as a military weapon, there is no evidence to support this; however, Dietrich Eckhart, a prominent Nazi with an interest in the occult, *did* search for religious artifacts, which may have been an inspiration for Lucas's storyline for *Raiders*.

Did the Ark of the Covenant ever exist and, if so, where is it now?

In this instance, history and movie fiction meld together and it's useful to separate the two.

Here's what we're told in the movie:

1. The Ark contains the fragments of the Ten Commandments as handed from God to Moses.
2. The Ark's final resting place is in Egypt, in a place called the Well of Souls.
3. The Ark has enormous power, capable of leveling armies. For that reason, it is coveted by Hitler who wants to harness its awesome power to make him invincible. Quite simply, Hitler sees this historical artifact as the means by which he can conquer the world.
4. The Ark is man's means of communicating with God.

Let's establish what we do know about it.

According to the Bible (Exodus 25:10–22), God commanded Moses to build an ark, giving very specific instructions. Its purpose was to be the physical interface between God and Moses, the mechanism by which He would give commandments to the children of Israel. Inside the ark were the broken pieces of the Ten Commandments.

The ark was made from acacia wood with a cover of pure gold on which two cherubim face each other. Here's what the Bible tells us about its dimensions: "two cubits and a half shall be its length, a cubit and a half its breadth, and a cubit and a half its height."

In the ark, spake God, "you shall put the testimony that I shall give you. There I shall meet with you, and from above the mercy seat, from between the two cherubim that are upon the ark of the testimony, I will speak with you of all that I will give you in commandment for the people of Israel."

The Ark of the Covenant is the object that everyone is
pursuing in the first movie. (Prop replica by Anthony Magnoli)

So we have biblical references to the Ark, but it raises the question:
Where *is* the Ark? Well, though there have been claims recently that it
has been found and there's a lot of speculation on where it currently
resides, the fact remains that no one knows for sure.

As Dr. Eric H. Cline points out in "Raiders of the Faux Ark," it's
important to separate fact from fancy, and attention should be paid to
those in the field with solid academic credentials instead of amateurs with
little (or no) credentials bankrolled by a gullible public who will appar-
ently believe anything if it's stated baldly and with a straight face, in a
search for these high-visibility artifacts.

To all those who open their purses to pay for those wild goose chases:
There are plenty of colleges and universities that do legitimate research
that could use your donations. Don't line the pockets of the opportunists
who are out there to make a fast buck at your expense, when funding for
legitimate research goes begging.

Is Major Toht's behavior consistent with Nazi history, or is he merely a stereotyped movie villain?

When Marion Ravenwood initially sees Major Arnold Toht (played by the late Ronald Lacey), she's characteristically fearless and confrontational, as is her style. Major Toht is obviously German, so Marion derisively calls him "Wehrmacht," which actually refers to the German armed forces, its army, navy, and air force, but not its elite Waffen-SS, the most dreaded of Hitler's troops. "Fraulein, let me show you what I am used to," Major Toht says, as he pulls a red-hot poker from the fire and holds it up to her face. Marion, quickly and wisely, changes her tune and is prepared to spill the beans.

Though he's a major, he wears no insignia, so we can't tell for certain what his Nazi affiliation is. In fact, the small Nazi pin on the lapel of his jacket is the only visible sign of his party affiliation. But given that he's obviously practiced in torture techniques, he is most likely a member of the Waffen-SS, the feared police force lead by Heinrich Himmler. The elite SS troops wore the death's head insignia, a skull, on the lapels of their uniforms. A remorseless lot, the police force routinely used torture to extract information, so it's not surprising that Major Toht quickly dispenses with the pleasantries with Marion and gets to the point, using the tip of a red-hot poker.

In the Nepalese bar, the Raven Saloon, Marion drinks a heavyset man under the table. Given that they consumed identical amounts of liquor, what is the likelihood that a woman with a smaller body mass could drink under the table a man with a higher body mass?

Although tolerance to alcohol and genetic factors can weigh heavily in one's favor, and although the number of drinks is not necessarily an accurate barometer of one's state of drunkenness, the fact remains that Marion Ravenwood is *half* the body mass of her drinking opponent, and would therefore be *much* more likely to be the first to go under the table.

There are fifteen shot glasses in front of them, each filled with hard liquor.

As Marion downs the last shot glass, her eyes wearily close; clearly, she's had enough. Just as the crowd thinks she's lost the contest, she yells out,

"Pistari! Pistari!" (It means "slowly, slowly" in Nepalese, the local dialect.) She's telling the onlookers, who have bet on the outcome, not to jump to conclusions. She then confidently plunks down the shot glass and watches her opponent fumble-fingering a shot glass. His face wreathed in a beautiful smile, he falls backward and Marion is victorious!

So could Marion really drink her opponent under the table?

Not bloody likely. Even after ten drinks, her blood alcohol percentage would be (based on 140 pounds) .32, but her opponent, weighing 240 pounds, would have had a blood alcohol percentage of .16, or about half of Marion's.

Given that they downed an estimated fifteen glasses of hard liquor, it's almost certain that the man would have drunk Marion under the table.

In 1936, how much was Marion asking in 2007 dollars for the headpiece?

Marion haggles with Indiana Jones for the headpiece, instrumental in finding the location of the Lost Ark of the Covenant. She demands $3,000 and Indy agrees; he offers another $2,000 to sweeten the deal. She agrees to $5,000.

That $5,000 would equal $71,000 in today's dollars. Obviously, Marion's not shy about demanding top dollar! And no wonder Indy was a little short on cash. Who walks around with *that* kind of money?

Is alcohol really flammable?

Yes. Its base is ethanol, which is commonly called alcohol.

In a riveting barroom scene, Indy is trying to save Marion Ravenwood while fighting off Major Toht and his three henchmen. At one point, Indy's head is pinned to the bar, as Major Toht gleefully ignites alcohol that blazes a trail toward Indy's head.

Was Hitler obsessed with the occult?

Nope. When historians look for information about connections between Hitler and the occult, there's no evidence to suggest Hitler embraced it; more to the point, there's nothing to suggest he was in search of religious artifacts. But there was another high-placed Nazi, Dietrich

Eckhart, who not only believed in the occult but was a practicing magician. Eckhart was also a member of the Thule Society and, as such, believed in the existence of a highly intelligent super race who could imbue others with power, thus creating Aryan supermen capable of exterminating lesser (i.e., tainted) species.

A cute capuchin monkey shows unusual intelligence, working on behalf of his master, a Nazi sympathizer. Are capuchin monkeys as intelligent as all that?

The monkey in the movie could have been trained to salute (heil, Hitler!), but other actions, such as distinguishing between good and bad guys or alerting the Nazis to Marion's hidden presence in a basket, are real stretches of imagination.

Of the New World monkeys in South America, capuchins are considered the most intelligent, especially the tufted capuchin, who, like his larger brethren, has used stones as tools to smash and crush food.

As for monkey business, research conducted at the Yale–New Haven hospital sheds new light on the admittedly adorable creature. "When taught to use money, a group of capuchin monkeys responded quite rationally to simple incentives; responded irrationally to risky gambles; failed to save; stole when they could; used money for food and, on occasion, sex." The researchers concluded that they behaved "a good bit" like another species . . . *Homo sapiens.*

Indy's friend Sallah peers down into an Egyptian tomb and sees the floor writhing with snakes. "Asps," he notes. "Very dangerous." How dangerous are asps? Are there any other snakes that Indy needs to watch out for in Egypt?

"Asp" is a generic, not taxonomic, term for a variety of venomous snakes, which is why a biologist would not refer to any specific snake as an asp. The word is thought to be a short form of *Vipera aspis,* or the Egyptian cobra. There are many other venomous snakes in Egypt, including the Puff Adder, the Black Desert Snake, and several species of vipers.

One of the most notorious venomous snakes (though it's not found in Egypt) is the King cobra, which has a distinctive hood framing its face.

Though it generally will not attack unless provoked, people rightly fear this snake. It can be up to seventeen feet in length and its venom has a high level of toxicity; if untreated after a bite, a person will die in approximately half an hour.

So Sallah is right. "Asps" *are* very dangerous, which is why he cheerfully lets Indy go first.

Did the Nazis have flying wing technology?

Yes, but not in time to influence the outcome of the war. At the behest of Luftwaffe commander Hermann Wilhelm Goering, flying wing technology was developed by two brothers, Reimar and Walter Horten. The initial design resembled a boomerang. Subsequent designs, including the twin propeller–driven single-seat Ho V built in 1942, took flight. (A flying wing is so named because it lacks a plane's traditional fuselage and tail.)

Clearly, though, the evolution of fighter aircraft would necessarily include jet engines, so a six-engined flying-winged Horten XVIII was developed for use as a long-range bomber. (It actually bears a striking resemblance to the U.S. stealth aircraft, the B-2.)

Further development lead to the Ho IX, the world's first jet-powered flying wing, which actually went into production after a successful test flight in January 1945, but it never took to the skies in combat because Allied forces subsequently overran the assembly plant. Four months later, on May 8, 1945, the Germans surrendered, rendering further development moot.

Once the Ark of the Covenant is discovered—thanks to Indy, not Belloq—the rush is on to get it to Germany, to Adolf Hitler. The plan is to transport it by air, by flying wing, a then-radical aircraft design.

In the Indy movie, the flying wing is not jet-powered but propeller-driven. As the Indy movie is set in 1936, that was well before the time that German research began on "flying wing" technology.

Amazingly, Indy is hanging onto a German sub that makes its way from a port in northern Egypt to a little island east of Sicily, the "football" being punted by boot-shaped Italy. Given that Indy could only survive the trip if the submarine never submerged, what are the odds the sub would have traveled topside for the entire trip?

Not likely. A German U-boat (*unterseeboot*, which means "undersea boat") is roughly three stories high and the length of a city block (252 feet), so it makes a great target for airplanes when it's above the waterline. Though a U-boat could conceivably defend itself with antiaircraft guns and a deck gun, its best defense is to run deep and hide in the depths of the ocean. Run silent, run deep is the motto of submariners everywhere, which is why it's often called the silent service.

A U-boat sitting topside is very vulnerable to attack from the air (planes), from the sea (ships), and from beneath the sea (other submarines). The best chance for survival is to surface only when absolutely necessary.

In other words, the submarine would routinely travel underwater for most of its journey, surfacing only to use the periscope, in which case, Indy would have drowned early in its journey.

Does the U.S. Army have a top-secret storage facility?

At the beginning of the movie, army intelligence officers promise that, when they're finished with the Ark, they'll return it to the university to be included in its archaeological holdings. But given its limitless power, the Ark is instead boxed up, stenciled with an inventory number, and deposited deep in the bowels of a cavernous storage building, where it will never again see the light of day.

When queried by Indy about the Ark's location, the army intelligence officers tell him that "top men" are working on it as they speak.

The U.S. military has three levels of security classification: confidential, secret, and top secret. The Ark, because of its destructive powers, would obviously be handled as a top-secret item, which means that IF it existed, it probably would be hidden away, underground, in a massive vault with armed guards on an around-the-clock basis.

But does the army actually *have* such a facility? As a former army officer with top-secret clearance, here's what I can tell you: Even if I *did* know about a secret warehouse hideaway, I could not confirm or deny its existence. Everything classified by the military is on a need-to-know basis; that is, if you are working on the project, you obviously have a "need to know." But if you're just curious, you don't have a *military* need to know, and hence the information cannot be shared with you. In fact, I could not tell you even if I wanted to.

For instance, let's say you have an interest in the top-secret air force base nicknamed Area 51, which is presumed to hold the physical remains of a UFO crash—the vehicle itself and the occupants. Is that true? Who knows? I don't. (I will tell you this: I was once stationed at an air force base in Nevada—I won't tell you which one—and I brought up this subject. I asked, "Just what kind of aliens are we harboring at Area 51?" It got a big laugh from all the other officers present.)

Bottom line: Don't ask about top-secret matters because I won't tell—I *can't* tell. (And no, I wouldn't have to kill you just because you asked—that's just another Hollywood misconception.)

One of the many colorful faces that greets the visitors to Adventureland. (Magic Kingdom, Walt Disney World, Orlando, Florida)

INDIANA JONES AND THE TEMPLE OF DOOM: CHINA AND INDIA, 1935

The movie opens with a protracted scene in Shanghai, at the Obi Wan club. Is there such a bar in China?

Not in Shanghai, which is where Club Obi Wan in the movie is. (Savvy *Star Wars* fans will catch the allusion: Obi Wan is a reference to Ben Kenobi, known as Obi Wan Kenobi, who introduces young Luke Skywalker to the Force.)

The real-world Club Obi Wan is located in the Xicheng district of Beijing. In addition to a full complement of drinks, both alcoholic and nonalcoholic, there's American-style food: chicken nuggets, lamb kebab, steak, spaghetti, subs, and salads. Housed in a three-level building, the

Indy holds the bad guys at bay with a machine gun in the marketplace scene re-creation. (Indiana Jones Stunt Spectacular, Walt Disney World, Orlando, Florida)

second floor offers a café, bar, and lounge, and the third floor is its rooftop patio with a great view of the Xihai lakeside.

Of course, it'd be really cool if the bar had been in existence *before* the Indiana Jones movie came out, but alas, it came *after* its release, and specifically cited the movie as the origin of its name.

Still, if you make it to Beijing, you can always pick up a few souvenirs and, when you get home, casually let it drop in conversation around the water cooler that you had dinner at Club Obi Wan in China. Chances are they won't know anything about it, and you'll be free to inflate the truth a bit: perhaps a little anecdote about a leggy showgirl with whom you had to escape to avoid capture by a Chinese gang, or perhaps a purchase on the black market brokered by some local characters of shady nature. Have fun improvising, but be *sure* to whip out a matchbook cover, napkin, or other branded souvenir that shows you really *did* go to Club Obi Wan. Tell 'em Lao Che sent you. . . .

A key plot point revolves around a jade urn carrying the ashes of Nurhachi, the first emperor of the Manchu Dynasty. Was there such a dynasty and such a person?

Yes to both. The Manchu Dynasty, known as the Qing Dynasty, held sway over China in the early sixteen hundreds. It was, in fact, China's last dynasty; afterward, the Republic of China was established, followed by the current PRC (People's Republic of China).

The movie refers to Nurhachi, the first emperor of that dynasty.

Was cremation common in China?

According to the *Encyclopedia of Cremation,* edited by Douglas J. Davies with Lewis H. Mates, "In China, cremation can be dated from the New Stone Age, 8,000–10,000 years ago." Throughout China's history, though, cremation varied in favor, depending on the dynasty. For instance, during the Tang Dynasty (618–907), the encyclopedia informs us, the Chinese "regarded cremation as a heresy." Later, however, in southeastern China, during the Song Dynasty, "cremation became traditional."

During the rule of Tai Tsu (Nurhachi), the first emperor of the Manchu Dynasty, cremation certainly would not have happened, since a prohibition then existed and the "Ceremonial Rules stipulated that cremations were not suitable for subjects belonging to the 'Eight Banners,' with the exception of those who were poor and living far away and who therefore could not be brought home after their deaths. Those who broke the rules were punished accordingly."

So, if Lao Che didn't know his Chinese history, he could have been convinced that the small jade urn carried the ashes of the first emperor of the Manchu Dynasty. (Actually, given the small size of the urn, it wouldn't have been large enough to contain the ashes of the average human. Assuming that the emperor had been cremated, and assuming he was 150 pounds, he would have needed a significantly larger urn than the one Indy passed on a Lazy Susan to Lao Che.)

In the movie, Lao Che is a Chinese gangster with legitimate businesses through which he launders money. Who was the real Lao Che?

As far as I can tell, there was no prominent Chinese gangster in the 1930s with the name of Lao Che. In fact, the only reference I found of any note is a brand of flour manufactured by a mill in Shanghai at the turn of the twentieth century—a wholly legitimate operation. Lao Che was the brand name of the flour.

Indy and Willie Scott fall three floors after leaping through a window at Club Obi Wan. After falling through three awnings, they land unscathed in a car. Is that actually possible?

On the television show *Mythbusters,* they reenacted this with an articulated dummy and also with a stunt actor. Though the dummy was banged up pretty badly, the shock sensors installed throughout the body showed that the fall wouldn't be fatal. Maybe bruised or maybe a broken bone or two, depending on how they hit the awnings, but they would have survived. The trained stunt double, tethered by a bungee cord, survived intact without a scratch.

Important safety tip: At higher elevations with nothing to break the fall, the circumstances dramatically change. For instance, in an article in *National Geographic* (December 1960), Joseph W. Kittinger Jr. explains that after parachuting from 103,300 feet, he was at one point traveling at an astounding rate of 614 miles per hour, nearly the speed of sound.

Can you imagine what it would have been like to hit the earth at that speed? (Can you say terminal velocity?)

In one of the most riveting scenes in the movie, Indy, Short Round, and Willie Scott survive a fall from a plane by hanging onto a life raft that inflates, slows their descent, and then slams into a snow-covered mountaintop, which they ride to its base. Could they have survived the fall?

No. In episode 37 of *Mythbusters,* they had three test drops at two thousand feet, keeping in mind their original inspiration: *Temple of Doom.* The conclusion was that it would have been nearly impossible to rig it to float like a parachute with a rate of descent that would have enabled survival. So, as the Discovery Channel show gleefully exclaims, "Myth busted!"

Did the Sankara stones really exist?

At the heart of the Indy Jones movie are three Sankara stones, one of which is purloined from a local village. According to the shaman, a holy

Indy battles for possession of the Sankara stones with Thuggee cult leader Mola Ram in the second Indiana Jones movie. (Prop replica by Anthony Magnoli)

man in the village, Indiana Jones was sent by divinity to go to the Pankot palace and retrieve it.

Actually, there are no such things. Shankara, best known as a philosopher who is credited for being one of the pillars of modern Hinduism, has no connection with what is termed in the movie "Sankara stones."

India does, however, venerate sacred stones. In fact, the Salagrama Sila stone is venerated. According to www.agt-gems.com, "the sale or purchase of a Salagrama Sila is strictly prohibited. Anyone who attempts to determine the material value of a Salagrama Sila will live in hell until the end of the universe."

So, a word to the wise: Leave it the hell alone!

On the other hand, we are told, "anyone who sees, worships, or bows to a Salagrama Sila will receive the same piety as doing millions of sacrifices and giving millions of cows in charity."

Hmmm . . . eternal damnation . . . or salvation. Must . . . choose . . . wisely.

Indy, Willie, and Short Round are "guests" at the Pankot Palace, beneath which is an active Thuggee cult. Where is the Pankot Palace in India?

Though India is known for its palaces, there's no Pankot Palace per se. But the adventurous tourist will find plenty of palaces where they won't be taken (so to speak) for a ride; instead, heed the advice of Lonely Planet's

Mel Capper and Tom Hall, who told the *Guardian* newspaper that "Udaipur's Lake and City Palaces are romantic, incredible sights, and the old city is an astonishing, colourful maze of streets. The views from the city's many rooftop restaurants are a highlight for many visitors. Don't miss Jaipur's bazaars, the Palace of Winds and the Amber Fort. Ranthambore Wildlife Sanctuary is the place for tiger-spotting. Chittorgarh's Fort is a symbol of the former Rajput rulers of the country and is another essential stop in the region. While in Rajasthan, many travelers detour to Agra's Taj Mahal."

As for the Pankot Palace, which looks very real in the film, was that shot on location? Actually, no. According to Mark Cotta Vaz and Shinji Hata *(From Star Wars to Indiana Jones: The Best of the Lucasfilm Archives),* "because filming restrictions in India precluded finding and shooting a real location, it was decided to conjure up the exterior palace scenes with matte paintings." The final palace shot, we're told, began with sketches by Spielberg and ended with detailed, lifelike paintings by artists.

Did Willie spy giant vampire bats?

Willy, Indy, and Short Round are on elephants, making their way from the village to Pankot Palace, not under cover of darkness but in daylight, when Willy spies what she thinks are large birds in flight, but Indy corrects her. They are, he says, "giant vampire bats." Are they really?

No. The vampire bat is not indigenous to India but to the northern hemisphere, specifically, Central and South America. The bats, called *Desmodus rotundus,* are also small (about the size of an adult thumb), with a wingspan of eight inches.

Even the vampire bats' bloody namesake is misleading: These bats don't actually *suck* blood but, in fact, bite their prey and lap up the blood.

So, Indy misidentified what he saw over the skies of India, because they weren't giant vampire bats. (Vampire bats, it should be noted, sleep during the day. It's only at night that they hunt, usually flying three feet off the ground—not treetop height, as seen in the movie.)

For the record, the large "birds" filmed in the movie were actually fruit bats *(Eidolon helvum),* which measure up to six feet from wingtip to wingtip.

The area of the Pankot Palace, we are told, was a hotbed of activity for the Thuggee cult, which flourished in India in the 1800s. The Thuggees worshipped the Indian goddess Kali, a symbol of death and destruction. Is this fact or movie fiction?

A little of both. The cult did flourish in India and worship Kali, but not in elaborate rituals on the scale as shown in the movie.

Members of the Thuggee cult preyed on innocent travelers, often ingratiating themselves by citing that traveling in numbers was safer, thus lulling their victims into a false sense of security. The Thuggee, working with others in his cult, would then wait until the opportunity presented itself, or take the victim to a specific location, to strangle the victim with a noose or other implement, and then rob and bury the unlucky person.

Though figures of the number of victims vary widely—from tens of thousands to two million—the fact remains that there's no way of knowing with any accuracy how many lives were lost at the hands of this cult of bloodthirsty Kali worshippers.

The cult's bloody reign ended in 1928, after the governor general of India, Lord William Bentinck, actively began a campaign to hunt down and kill its members.

It should be noted that the Thuggee cult did not, as the movie portrays, rip human hearts out of their victims, nor manacle them in cages to be dropped into molten lava, incinerating them.

Indian food is, for most people, exotic fare, but the offerings at the dinner table in this movie were unique: large insects, monkey brains, and living snakes. Are these really the more exotic gustatory delights of native Indians?

Um, yes. In fact, Spielberg and Lucas had to tone down the gustatory delights to make it more palatable to the rest of us who eat more prosaic fare. In India, large insects are usually harvested during the fall, and the larger, the better, but freshness is an issue because the crunchy flavor is prized. Likewise, writhing snakes are preferred to dead ones because it's proof that the meat is fresh, which is also prized in Indian cuisine. Monkey brains, however, have fallen out of favor because of these politically correct times; the monkeys are on an endangered list in India, which has forced Indians to eat less exotic fare, like sheep's brains. Monkey brains are also considered aphrodisiacs.

Sorry, folks, I'm just kidding! I bet I had some of you guys convinced! But it makes me wonder how many people who have never had Indian cuisine decided *not* to eat any Indian food as a result of seeing this unappetizing movie.

The truth is that Indian food is delicious, and Indians eat pretty much what we eat, though prepared differently. (Curry is a favorite flavoring, though it is not to my taste.)

Main meat dishes typically include chicken, steak, prawn (shrimp to you), and lamb. Vegetarian dishes include curry, tomatoes, eggplant, and potato. Starch usually takes the form of steamed rice and bread, both served up in a variety of dishes.

Indians *do not* relish live snakes, monkey brains, soups with floating eyeballs, or chitinous insects at the dinner table, so don't bother to ask for them on the menu. The waiter will likely give you a quizzical look and go away muttering something about crazy Americans. And he'd be right to think so.

How hot does lava get? Would it melt a metal rack?

During a Thuggee ceremony, a metal torture rack, with a hapless victim inside (remember, his heart had previously been ripped out of his body), is lowered into a river of lava. The rack comes back up, but the victim does not.

Lava, depending on its source, can reach temperatures as high as 2,140 degrees Fahrenheit, according to Dr. Scott Rowland (University of Hawaii). At that temperature, some (but not all) metals melt. Since we don't know what the rack is constructed of, and since it didn't melt in the molten lava, we'd have to assume that it was a metal that could withstand the temperature, in which case I'd go with iron, which melts at 2,786 degrees Fahrenheit. But molten lava's pretty hot, so the rack might bend out of shape; however, the human sacrifice, strapped in and dunked in the fiery flow, would be burned alive.

INDIANA JONES AND
THE LAST CRUSADE:
VENICE, AUSTRIA, AND
ALEXANDRETTA, 1938

Is there a historical record of the Cross of Coronado? And who was Coronado?

The movie opens in 1912 with a young Indiana Jones, a Boy Scout, riding with his troop in Utah. He witnesses a band of thieves who discover the Cross of Coronado, but in real life there's no Cross of Coronado. The cross is simply a movie prop, constructed to resemble gold on one side and bejeweled on the reverse, with the image of a crucified Christ.

As for Coronado, he existed. A fifteenth-century Spanish explorer, Francisco Vasquez de Coronado and his troops searched parts of the American southwest (Arizona and New Mexico). They searched in vain for the Seven Cities of Gold, which according to Jay Miller (www.southernnewmexico.com) was likely folklore. "The Seven Cities of Gold has been a New Mexico fable since before Fray Marcos de Niza claimed to have seen them in 1539. As soon as Cortés and crew finished conquering the Aztec Empire in the early 1520s, they set out to find the legendary Seven Cities of Gold, said to have been established by seven bishops who fled Spain after the Moorish conquest to hide gold, gems, and religious articles in the New World."

Young Indy rescues the cross from the thieves but reluctantly surrenders it to the local sheriff, who promptly turns it over to the bandits. Their leader is not named but wears a trademark fedora hat, which he gives to Indy to show that he respects the boy's efforts.

Cut to 1938. On board a ship, Indy is battling with his old nemesis, played by actor Paul Maxwell, in an attempt to recover the cross. Indy does so, barely escaping the sinking ship—the Coronado.

▲

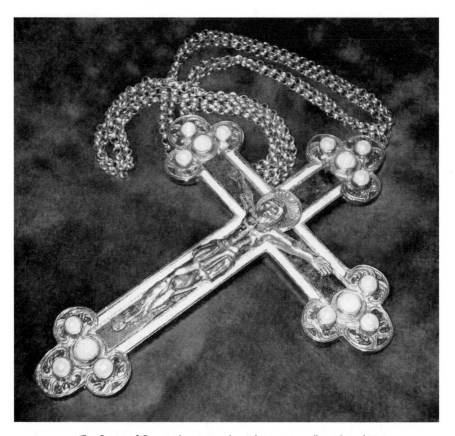

The Cross of Coronado was made with a pewter alloy, plated in brass, and aged. Weighing more than two pounds, it is based on the historic Cross of Justinian. (Prop replica by Anthony Magnoli)

In the movie, the legendary Holy Grail proves to be maddeningly elusive. Guarded by a knight, there's one true Grail . . . and many false ones. What, exactly, is the Holy Grail?

Grail legend draws from both Celtic and Christian origins and follows several trains of thought, including its literary origin in a story told by Chrétien de Troyes. But the version most people are familiar with is that told in *Joseph d'Arimathie,* in which Robert de Boron explains the Holy Grail as the chalice used by Christ at the Last Supper; after his crucifixion, it was used to collect his blood. Afterward, Joseph and his followers became custodians of the Holy Grail.

This is basically how the movie portrays it: as a physical object, a holy chalice with a profound religious connection to the Christian faith.

In a broader perspective, however, a Holy Grail, or a search for the Grail, is a personal quest for the unattainable.

As to the cup's actual existence, opinion is divided. Some believe it exists, citing possible locations where it's currently hidden, though that's the stuff of conspiracy theories. Most archaeologists believe it doesn't physically exist.

Brendan O'Neill, for BBC News, explored the subject in "The never-ending search" and collected various perspectives:

Eric Eve (a New Testament scholar at Oxford) explains, "In the version of the legend I know, the Grail is meant to be the chalice Jesus used at the Last Supper, subsequently brought to England by Joseph of Arimathea. But there is no first-century evidence about what happened either to the chalice or to Joseph—assuming he's even a historical character."

Richard Barber, author of *The Holy Grail: Imagination and Belief,* echoes Eve's opinion. "It is pure literature. It was imagined by a French writer . . . at the end of the twelfth Century, in the romance of Perceval. His vision is at the root of all the Grail stories."

And a former Bishop of Edinburgh concludes, "It's all good fun but absolute nonsense. The quest for the Holy Grail belongs with the quest for the ark Noah left on Mount Ararat or the fabled Ark of the Covenant Indiana Jones is always chasing."

In other words, it's a great story—but alas!—nothing more.

What is the story behind the Brotherhood of the Cruciform Sword's insignia? Did they, in fact, serve as guardians of the Holy Grail?

According to the film, the Brotherhood of the Cruciform Sword is a secret society that, over the centuries, has sought to protect the Holy Grail from those who seek it for their own ends.

The Brotherhood of the Cruciform is a fictional device. The design of the Brotherhood's symbol is a combination of a Latin cross and a chalice, which suggests the Holy Grail. As with the Brotherhood itself, the symbol has no historical basis in fact.

In the movie, Indy and Dr. Elsa Schneider discover the Tomb of St. Richard in a catacomb under a Venice library. Does Venice have catacombs?

No. If the movie is referring to St. Richard of Chichester, where miracles have supposedly occurred at his tomb, we have two problems, both geographical. First, St. Richard's tomb is located in Chichester cathedral in West Sussex, England, a good distance from Venice, which in the movie is where we are told the tomb is located. Second, Venice is an elevated city and, as such, could not and does not have catacombs.

In a critical chase scene, Indy is hanging onto the barrel of a side cannon on a tank. Was that just a movie prop or did the Germans actually have such tanks?

The Germans did, back in World War I. According to *From Star Wars to Indiana Jones,* "Only eight such tanks had actually been built for the war, and with the only surviving tank a nonfunctioning museum piece, mechanical effects supervisor George Gibbs and his crew had to construct their full-scale replica from scratch."

In the movie, Indy and his father escape from a German zeppelin by means of a biplane attached to its underside. Did the Germans use zeppelins in World War II and were there any planes attached underneath?

The zeppelin is named after its inventor, German Count Ferdinand von Zeppelin. Extensively used before World War I as the world's first commercial airline, the zeppelin reached its height of popularity and fame in 1929 when the *Graf Zeppelin* circled the world, starting from, and returning to, Lakehurst, New York.

During World War II, zeppelins in Germany were commandeered by the German Air Force's Hermann Goering for use as propaganda vehicles. In 1937, though, the zeppelin *Hindenburg,* filled with flammable hydrogen (instead of the rarer but safer helium gas), caught fire in its tail section. Thousands of spectators witnessed the horrific event of the *Hindenburg* crashing to the ground, killing twenty-two crew members and thirteen passengers.

As for the prospect of attaching planes beneath it, neither the *Graf Zeppelin* nor the *Hindenburg* were outfitted thus; however, there was a U.S. zeppelin, the *USS Akron,* that carried an internal hanger in which five airplanes were housed, each capable of being air-launched.

The Knights Templar are sometimes cited in connection with the Grail. What was their role in guarding the Grail through the ages?

In the film, an immortal knight, the last of three brothers, is guarding the Holy Grail. Here, we are dealing with myth. In one story, the Knights excavated the Grail and were supposed to have appointed themselves as its guardians for time immemorial, but there's no record in Knights Templar history of this story.

The Holy Grail cup rests on a stone tablet; both key elements of the third Indiana Jones movie. (Prop replicas by Anthony Magnoli)

In the movie, Indy has to pass three trials in order to gain access to the Inner Grail Temple. Do the three trials have any basis in fact?

In the film, the three trials included the breath of God (only a penitent man will pass), the word of God (follow in his footsteps), and the path of God (the leap from the lion's head).

The three trials make for great moviemaking, but there were in fact no such trials. The closest fact comes to fiction is the notion that in Grail legend, according to Malcolm Godwin, there must be a separation of ego from self before one can proceed. "Only through suffering and the twin agencies of doubt and love can this be transmuted into compassion," he explains in *The Holy Grail: Its Origins, Secrets, and Meaning Revealed.*

Indy's compassion, his impetus for finding the Grail, is not for himself but for his father, as Indy seeks its healing powers. Riddled with doubt when taking a leap of faith (stepping out onto what appears to be nothingness, where in fact a camouflaged path exists), Indy makes his way to the Inner Grail Temple, where he chooses wisely and picks the Holy Grail, filling it from a fount of water and returning to use it to heal his father's wound—the wounded king (the father) of which the Grail myth speaks.

INDIANA JONES AND THE KINGDOM OF THE CRYSTAL SKULL: 1950S

What exactly is the crystal skull and what place does it hold in archaeology?

Crystal skulls actually have more in common with discussions that center on things on the outer fringes of reality. The website www.mendhak.com discusses aliens, UFOs, prophecies, cryptozoology, parascience, conspiracies, mythologies, mysteries, ghosts, and other paranormal matters, unsolved mysteries, and unexplained phenomena.

Included in that rather curious but interesting mix is the matter of crystal skulls, which we're told is "One of archaeology's most compelling mysteries. . . . the thirteen crystal skulls. Skulls have been one of the most powerful objects of symbolism in human history, all over the world. Several 'perfect' crystal skulls have been found in parts of Mexico, Central and South America. . . . The skulls are believed to be between 5,000 and 35,000 years old."

According to this website, the skulls are significant because some believe that they possess "magical powers and healing properties"; yet others believe they "have the capability to enable us to look into the past, present, and future."

Since we know little about what aspect Lucas is exploring in this fourth movie, we can only speculate. We know, for instance, that the skull is rare and valuable, but that in and of itself would not be sufficient justification for the Soviets to be interested in it. What, then, accounts for their interest? My guess is that Lucas has chosen to explore its capabilities as a supernatural element of great power.

As is always the case when dealing with matters of history, the truth is out there; and sometimes, it's *way* out there. . . .

▲

PART 3

The Disney Connection and Dress for Success, Indiana Jones Style

A leering mask greets guests who enter Adventureland. (Magic Kingdom, Walt Disney World, Orlando, Florida)

EXPERIENCING THE INDIANA JONES ADVENTURE WORLDWIDE

As befitting his penchant for globetrotting, Indiana Jones—at least the Disney adventure experience—can be found worldwide, in California, Florida, Paris, and Tokyo.

Hang on. It's going to be a bumpy ride. . . .

But before you go, make sure you're properly dressed for the occasion. I have some wardrobe tips in case you don't know where to shop.

DISNEYLAND

The Indiana Jones Adventure: Temple of the Forbidden Eye

Opening date: March 3, 1995

Experience: "jungle transport" vehicle

Duration: 3 minutes, 15 seconds

Location in park: Adventureland

Tourist tip: Get a Fastpass for this ride; otherwise, you'll be waiting in line for at least an hour or two.

Background: In Hindu mythology, Mara, known as "Lord of the Senses," tried in vain to tempt Buddha with his three daughters (thirst, desire, and delight), but Buddha (of saintly persuasion) resisted. Disney Imagineer Tony Baxter was the project leader on this ride, which involved four hundred Imagineers, including a core team of one hundred.

The premise of this bumpy, jarring ride is that Mara, who will peer into your soul, will be granting you one of three boons: earthly riches, eternal youth, or future knowledge. So the theme is consistent with Hindu religion, since Mara's daughter Raga represents desire for things that we mere mortals have always sought, often in vain.

Getting *to* the temple, though, is no easy matter when there's a long line. As is always the case, Disney masterfully provides plenty of visual diversions

▲

long before you board the car: static displays of a pre–WW II encampment (with boxes appropriately stenciled "Dr. Jones"), a loading dock with a roped artifact waiting to be loaded, a generator noisily cranking away, and a well that warns you not to pull the rope (go ahead; it's part of the gag).

Once you enter the temple, however, it's still a bit of a walk to the actual transport loading station, but it's great fun. The cavern twists and turns, and though it's not recommended for people suffering from claustrophobia, it's lit (though dimly, with torches) and has several appropriately haunting displays, including scenes of an encampment, a room with deadly stakes (ascending and descending), and other grisly sights.

The waiting area shows a deliberately grainy, black-and-white newsreel narrated by a familiar figure: actor John Rhys-Davies in his role as Sallah, an Egyptian who helped Indy in the first movie. "I, Sallah, will give you counsel," he says, then provides safety tips for riding in the transport vehicle.

Each vehicle seats twelve riders, and it's a bumpy, jerky ride. You pass into the Chamber of Destiny and are scrutinized by the Eye of Mara, who randomly selects whether you are to be granted the boon of riches, youth, or knowledge. Immediately thereafter, the vehicle veers off on one of three tracks.

As with all Disney rides, the themed areas are designed to give you a carefully orchestrated visual, aural, and physical experience. In this case, after passing through the Chamber of Destiny, you venture through the Hall of Promise, the Tunnel of Torment, Gates of Doom, the Cavern of

Bubbling Death, the Mummy Chamber, the Bug Room, a Snake Temple, a Rat Cave, a Dart Corridor (you can feel blasts of air simulating the blown darts, with accompanying sound), and (you guessed it) a Rolling Boulder experience that'll have you ducking!

As the ride is very jerky, with sudden movements, I found it best to hold onto the handles in front of me, relax, and just go with the flow.

Afterward, be sure to stop by the gift shop and pick up a souvenir. (You can't go wrong with one of the baseball caps, as one size fits all and there are several eye-catching designs.)

DISNEY WORLD

The Indiana Jones Stunt Spectacular

Opening date: August 25, 1989

Experience: sit-down, covered amphitheater; seats 2,000. Live-action stunt show.

Duration: approximately 30 minutes

Location in park: Disney's Hollywood Studios

Tourist tip: get a Fastpass as soon as you get in the park, and then return at the appropriate time.

Useful tips: The show starts seating twenty minutes before showtime. Because of the design (curved seating with rising tiers), there are no bad seats in the house. This show also picks members of the audience to be part of the show, under the tutelage of a cast member. (You have to be at least eighteen years old. To increase your chances of getting picked, sit near the front row, wear colorful clothing, and show a *lot* of spirit and excitement. They pick only ten people.)

Fun fact: The sets, which are moved between scenes, weigh an astonishing one hundred tons each.

Drawing entirely from the first film, this show highlights three key scenes. From its opening sequence, Indy snatches the golden idol and nearly gets bowled over; from a scene in Cairo, Indy cracks his whip to hold off the bad guys as Indy and Marion scamper up a building and escape using a long pole; and Indy fist-fights with a towering man, a Nazi mechanic, as his fellow soldiers prepare to fly a plane carrying the Ark to Berlin.

Towering over the entrance, the figure of Indiana Jones wielding
his trademark whip commands the attention of passersby.
(Indiana Jones Stunt Spectacular, Walt Disney World, Orlando, Florida)

Of course, if you've seen the first film, you think that you know what's going to happen, but you would be wrong. There are some surprises.

The show is fast paced with fires, explosions, and the guns, so you have to pay close attention to take it all in. There is also lots of spirited dialogue and visual gags.

You'll walk away from this one with a big grin on your face and want to go back, time and again. This show is definitely a crowd pleaser!

Gift Store

Near the amphitheater, you'll find the Indiana Jones Adventure Outpost Store. There you'll find the most complete selection of Indy product in the world. (The closest runner-up: the gift store at Disneyland when exiting the ride The Indiana Jones Adventure: Temple of the Forbidden Eye.)

Important tip: Although there is some Indiana Jones product at the flagship store in Orlando at the Disney Marketplace, the theme park has a wider selection. It's an incentive to get "guests" (as Disney calls the customers) into the theme park. If nothing else, buy an inexpensive souvenir

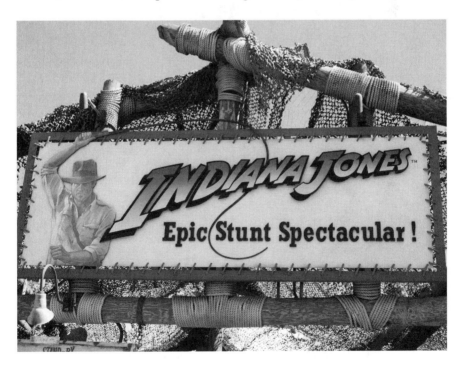

like a baseball cap. It's only $20 and essential to protect yourself from the relentless Florida sun.

DISNEYLAND RESORT PARIS

Indiana Jones and the Temple of Peril

Opening date: 1993

Experience: "mine cars" on a roller-coaster ride with a loop

Duration: 1 minute, 15 seconds

Sacre bleu! This is an open air roller-coaster ride appropriate for the entire family, but thrill junkies will prefer the faster, higher, scarier, and more convoluted roller coasters—the heart-stopping, adrenaline-pumping, eye-popping, gravity-defying experience that makes you feel wonderfully alive!

A static display set up in the passageway of the "Temple of the Forbidden Eye"; digging tools, manuscripts, and field journals with detailed drawings attest to the rigors of archaeology. (Indiana Jones Adventure—"The Eye of Mara," Disneyland, Anaheim, California)

Indiana Jones Adventure: Temple of the Crystal Skull

Opening date: Spring 1993

Experience: oversized jeeps on a preprogrammed path

Duration: 3 minutes

Rising above the trees, the ruins of an ancient Aztec jungle command your attention. As you draw near, you pass an imaginatively designed environment with an abandoned hangar, an archaeological dig in progress, a single-engine seaplane (marked "C-3PO"), and erected tents, and cross a wooden bridge. In the area where you wait in line for the ride, the interior walls of a pyramid are magnificently decorated with elaborate carvings.

Entering the Chamber of Purity, you are surrounded by pools and grottos. Most prominent of all: the crystal skull that menacingly glows, emanating powerful rays from its eye sockets. To evade its effects, your jeep suddenly speeds up and continues on its path through caverns and chambers filled with . . . well, let me not spoil the surprise but allow you to take the ride yourself as I wish you good day and a safe journey.

An archaeologist's tent is his castle; a static display representative of his home away from home. (Indiana Jones Adventure—" The Eye of Mara," Disneyland, Anaheim, California)

THE GREAT MOVIE RIDE

Movie fans don't want to miss one of the best attractions at Disney's Hollywood Studios in Orlando: The Great Movie Ride. Located inside a reproduction of Mann's Chinese Theatre, the ride debuted in May 1989. It's a must for any movie fan. The lines are often long, but there's plenty to capture your attention as you wait for the tram: authentic movie memorabilia on display (including a pair of Dorothy Gale's ruby slippers) and, in the waiting area, vintage movie clips on a large movie screen.

The ride itself uses Disney's Audio-Animatronics to bring to life the most memorable scenes in movie history, from Gene Kelly in *Singin' in the Rain* to Sigourney Weaver in *Alien*. To add a little spice to the ride, the tram is hijacked by either a gangster or a cowboy in an elaborate and satisfying visual gag with a spectacular ending.

As for the Indy connection, he makes an appearance in a reenacted scene along with Sallah, as they raise the Ark of the Covenant from its resting place, the Well of Souls. Since *Raiders of the Lost Ark* is such an iconic film, it would have been odd indeed if the Imagineers who dreamed up this attraction had left him out!

DRESSING AND
LOOKING THE PART

Let's face it, if you're an armchair traveler, chances are you won't find yourself gingerly making your way through a steamy jungle in South America with a native guide urging you on. Even so, you enjoy watching the movies and want to show your true colors, so you ask: What Indiana Jones geek wear is available?

Indiana Jones T-shirts are offered for sale at the Indiana Jones Adventure Outpost at Disney's Hollywood Studios, located within the Walt Disney World Resort.

T-shirts. You can't go wrong with a licensed T-shirt, of which there are many designs from all three films. To promote the fourth film, there are two different designs: a black T-shirt and a white T-shirt, both bearing the legend "Indiana Jones and the Kingdom of the Crystal Skull." Both are available exclusively from http://shop.starwars.com and cost $16.99.

Headgear. You have two choices: a wide selection of baseball caps, or the traditional fedora hat. Of the two, you're probably better off going with the baseball cap, since it can be worn daily, and it's practically part of the uniform of any American tourist.

The fedora, however, is limited to men, and let's be honest, you have to be a rugged, manly man to wear it with brio. Otherwise, it looks, well, a little out of place. Still, if you can pull it off, the official Lucasfilm shop online has two different designs: a brown hat (for adventures) and a black hat (for more formal occasions).

In the marketplace battle, Marion escapes to safety by sliding down a fortuitously positioned rope. (Indiana Jones Stunt Spectacular, Walt Disney World, Orlando, Florida)

Most folks, however, will opt for a baseball cap. Great for year-round use and especially handy when you're visiting one of the Disney theme parks. (Please try to avoid looking *too* touristy with Mickey Mouse ears or a Mickey Mouse cap.)

The Indiana Jones baseball caps are really quite stylish. Available in brown, beige, and tan colors, the price is $15.99, which is reasonable. (I paid a couple bucks more at Disney World for one of the caps.)

Now, for that authentic Indiana Jones look, here's what you need, and where you'll need to go.

Fedora. Though there are several vendors offering knockoffs (ranging from inexpensive to pricey), your best bet is to buy an officially licensed fedora that looks exactly like the movie version. In this regard, the vendor of choice is www.thefedorastore.com, where a wool felt fedora is $57.95, though they sometimes have a sale price of $44.95. With its grosgrain trim, 2⅜-inch brim, distressed vintage look, and dusted finish, this is perfect headgear for any chisel-jawed man with steely eyes who knows how to wear such a hat with aplomb and a straight face.

Leather jacket. This will be the most expensive item in your wardrobe, so you don't want to skimp on it. The vendor of choice is the Wested Leather Company located in Swanley, Kent, England.

As Wested Leather Company's owner, Peter Botwright, explains on his website (www.wested.com), "In 1980 I was commissioned to design and make the Indiana Jones jacket for the film *Raiders of the Lost Ark*. The jacket passed through many stages of design, finally meeting the exact requirements of both the film's designers and Mr. Harrison Ford himself."

Due to currency fluctuations, the cost of the jacket varies; at this writing, the cost is £295. For that money, however, what you get is a handcrafted replica jacket made from the finest, soft English lambskin, with two-way pockets, action pleats for arm movement, side vents, and a leather-bound inside pocket.

A versatile article of clothing, a leather jacket is perfect for outdoor wear in the most rugged of circumstances, from negotiating a dank cave with nasty spiders dropping on you, to covering the shoulders of a beautiful

young woman who needs sheltering from the rain. (Go ahead and show your chivalrous nature. It always pays off with the dames.)

Boots. As the saying goes, the shoes make the man, and that's certainly true of Indiana Jones, who relies on his durable, comfortable boots to carry him through thick and thin.

The vendor who made Indy's boots is Alden Shoe Company (aldenshoe.com) in New England. Their model #405 is the actual boot worn by Indy. An exceptionally sturdy work boot, these boots are made for walking and can take a lot of abuse. On the company's website, one of the customers posted a photo of his well-worn, distressed #405s, noting, "They've been with me through seven or eight countries and an archaeological dig. I'm finally getting the heels replaced after two years." Expect to pay about $300 a pair.

Whip. Frankly, I can't imagine why the average Indiana Jones fan would need this item. It can be a dangerous, even lethal, weapon and therefore must be used with caution. That said, if you're in character and in costume as Indy, you *definitely* need a whip, and www.davidmorgan.com is the place to get one, because David Morgan is the guy who designed and manufactured the whips actually used in the Indiana Jones films.

Available only online, a replica whip runs $840, but with care, it lasts a lifetime. (It's perfect for those moments when you need to get out of a tight spot: when you are cornered by a lion, find yourself needing to swing across an abyss or stream, need to snatch a gun out of the hands of one of your guides who's had a change of heart and wants to perforate you, or need a new method of persuasion to whip your hubby back in line.)

Safety note: If you've not used a whip before, make sure you buy a "how to" video, so you know how to handle it correctly and won't hurt anyone. Handling a whip seems intuitive, but it takes a lot of practice to become skilled in its use.

Bag, belt. You can look the part but you need to accessorize for maximum effect. For a distressed leather bag or WWII vintage British Mark VII gas-mask bag, both of which Indy used, a good source is Todd's Costumes (www.toddscostumes.com), where movie replicas are made for a reasonable cost.

In addition to bags, this company sells Indy-inspired shirts, fedoras, leather straps, gloves, holsters, gun and web belts, and whip holders. From the looks of it, the replicas are pretty convincing. Men will definitely take to the "Indiana Jones" style shirt ($58), which is a "basic khaki 'safari' shirt." According to Todd's Costumes, its features include: "long-staple cotton that will wash up with the proper wrinkly look; shoulder epaulets; pleats down the front; matching color buttons; wide-bodied loose fit." Just the thing for wear in the Amazonian jungle and the concrete jungle, too.

General vintage clothing. Magnoli Clothiers (www.magnoliclothiers.com) is an Internet-only clothing store that specializes in "tailor-made clothing and footware in vintage styles from the 1930s and 1940s. We also stock a range of custom-made accessories, such as leather-bound journals, cuff links, and vintage style ties."

Anthony "Indy" Magnoli, best known for his movie prop replicas, has turned his attention to high-quality, individually made, tailored clothing that hearkens back to a time when people dressed fashionably. The line includes hats, suits, jackets, tuxedos, shirts, pants, footwear, leather garments, overcoats, vests, ties, accessories, and journals.

The Magnoli line is for men only (unfortunately), but for those men who want to avoid the contemporary American look (jeans, T-shirts, and sneakers) and catch the attention of the dames, Magnoli Clothiers can outfit you as a man of the world, rather than an ambulatory billboard for licensed apparel.

PART 4

Ports of Call for the Intrepid: Locations by Movie

"GEORGE HAS NEVER STOPPED ASKING, 'ANY IDEAS?' AND

THE WHOLE WORLD HAS BEEN A BETTER PLACE FOR IT.

FOR TWO DECADES I'VE TRIED TO UNEARTH IT AS IF IT

WERE SOME ARCHAEOLOGICAL ANTIQUITY—GEORGE

LUCAS'S CRYSTAL BALL."

—Steven Spielberg, in the foreword to Charles
Champlin's *George Lucas: The Creative Impulse*

Although movies are shot on location all over the world, cost and access are key considerations, so directors prefer sites that are geographically closer to their home bases. And in cases where local access is denied, environments are recreated on large sound stages, aided by exquisitely detailed matte paintings that look convincingly real.

For the Indiana Jones movies, footage has been shot all over the world. Some of the places are instantly recognizable, but others are not as well known. In any case, if you want to get a feel for the world of Indiana Jones, it pays to take a trip and retrace his steps. You'd be surprised where they've shot some of the scenes.

Remember the first movie and the lush subtropical environment? Isn't that how you'd envision South America? Most people would, but very few people—unless they knew its actual filming location—would know where Indy was nearly flattened by a giant boulder. (Hint: you can go there and get "leid.")

Let me take you behind the scenes, so to speak, and point out a few places where Indy *really* traveled to, so you can follow in his oversized, adventurous footsteps.

RAIDERS OF THE LOST ARK

As the movie opens, we see Indy making his way through a lush South American rain forest. Actually, Indy is making his way on one of the Hawaiian islands, specifically, **Kauai,** at its fabled **Fern Grotto,** which is described by wailuabay.com as "a natural amphitheater fringed with hanging ferns and lush plant life."

Because it's reasonably close to California but still looks like a remote destination, Kauai is a favorite place to shoot footage, according to *National Geographic,* which cites three other famous films the island has hosted: *South Pacific, King Kong* (Dino de Laurentiis's 1976 version), and *Jurassic Park.*

The **Huleia Stream,** says the magazine, is "where jungle greenery grows to the water's edge. This lush landscape appeared in the Indiana Jones movie *Raiders of the Lost Ark.*"

The scene in which Professor Indiana Jones is teaching a class on archaeology, mostly to dreamy-eyed coeds who obviously have little interest in the subject matter, is on the fictional campus of **Barnett College** in New York. (One coed, anxious to get her interest in the professor across in an obvious manner, has penciled her eyelids with the words, "LOVE YOU," which he reads, finding himself temporarily distracted from his lecture.)

Though there is a real-world college similarly named (Barnet College in London), this particular classroom is also located in England, at the **Royal Masonic School for Girls** in Rickmansworth Park, Rickmansworth, Hertfordshire.

When in Egypt, Indy stays at his friend Sallah's house. This house can be found in **Tunisia** (where *Star Wars* was filmed), in the city of **Kairouan.** (And, no, the city's name doesn't translate to Cairo.) Actually, Kairouan is the holiest city in Tunisia. The city is located due east of the country's center point.

The famous fight scenes (Indy fighting the Nazis and the local bad guys, including the menacing swordsman) were also filmed in Kairouan.

Indy finds himself at a Nazi dig (the Tannis Development) in Cairo, Egypt, where the search is on for the Lost Ark of the Covenant. The real-world location where this major scene was shot can be found in **Tozeur, Tunisia,** located in the western part of the country.

There's really not much digging going on in search of Egyptian tombs and artifacts in this city, where tourism is its principal business, despite its extreme heat, which averages over 110 degrees in the summer and fall. (Important safety tip: wear a hat, put on sunscreen, and bring plenty of bottled water.)

West of Tozeur, **Nefta** is the location where Indy and Marion find themselves battling Nazis as they attempt to destroy a flying wing aircraft that the Nazis hoped would be used to transport the captured Ark of the Covenant to Berlin. Of course, the Nazis fail miserably and are forced to take the Ark by truck convoy on the first leg of the trip. (That reminds me: Like the indigenous people seen in the first part of the movie, the Nazis are terrible shots when it comes to hitting Indy. Marksmanship classes are needed all round, folks.)

The scenery in Nefta should look pretty familiar to Indy fans, since the riveting scene with the truck chase was filmed here as well.

When you think of **La Rochelle, France,** chances are you know it as a beautiful seaport in western France. During World War II, however, the Nazis built a submarine pen at its main port, La Pallice. The sub pen, still standing but not in use, was also used in the movie *Das Boot,* which is about a German U-boat.

The footage of the ship *Bantu Wind,* commanded by Captain Katanga, was also shot here in La Rochelle.

The last city in France to be liberated, it once held an estimated 20,000 German troops. Now the picturesque city is known for its splendid seafood restaurants, recreational boating, and beautiful countryside.

At the end of the film, the Nazis set up a hidden base on one of the remote **Cyclades islands** of Greece. But don't go there looking for the scene in the movie, which was shot in the United States at a wildlife refuge near San Francisco. (Remember, shooting on location is expensive and problematic, so filmmakers always prefer to shoot in and around California.)

A friendly face "greets" visitors to Adventureland. (Magic Kingdom, Walt Disney World, Orlando, Florida)

INDIANA JONES AND THE TEMPLE OF DOOM

The film's opening was shot in the **Rua da Felicidade** in Macau, of which government officials say: "Once the commercial hub of Macau, this network of alleys form the core of the old Inner Harbour District. Most of the buildings stand just two to three stories high, with those in Rua da Felicidade highly prized and preserved for their historic connections."

If you want a wild time, check out **Club Obi Wan,** a bar in **Beijing, China.** Its owners tells us that it promotes "a gastronomic and nightlife concept of diversity integrated in one place. . . . To all you movie freaks out there, the derivation of Club Obi Wan's name won't come as a surprise to you."

No surprise, and the club's menu is mundane fare, obviously Americanized: potato chips, fried mushrooms, soup, bruschetta, salads, sub sandwiches, spaghetti, seafood, chicken nuggets, and steak. The dessert, however, is a little odd for American tastes: pancakes topped with your choice of banana, chocolate, honey, jelly, or peanut butter. (What? No maple syrup?)

In other words, you can't get pigeons flambé, which is what Indy uses to spear one of the Chinese gangsters.

When Indy, Willie, and Short Round cleverly elude the very long arm of Chinese gangster Lao Che, they board a cargo plane at the Nang Tao airport that, unbeknownst to them, actually belongs to Lao Che Air Freight. A hangar in the background bears the legend "Pan American Airways System." Though Pan Am is long gone, the hangar and the airport actually exist. Both of them can be found at California's **Hamilton Air Force Base,** decommissioned in 1974, and permanently closed in 1988 by the BRAC (Base Realignment and Closure) Commission. It's currently under the control of the city of Novato and the county of Marin, not far from George Lucas's Skywalker Ranch.

▲

In one of the most harrowing scenes, Indy and company are riding—hanging on for dear life, actually—a yellow raft and are propelled at high speed over a towering cliff, but you don't have to go to India to see that cliff. Instead, go to the **Snake River Canyon in Twin Falls, Idaho,** where the scene was filmed.

Out of the frying pan and into the fire, so to speak: Indy, Willie, and Short Round miraculously survive a fall from a plane, only to hit a snow-covered slope, rush downhill at breakneck speed, and catapult off a cliff, after which they land upright and must negotiate whitewater rapids in India.

Though whitewater rafting expeditions in India are among the world's best, Indy fans wanting to replicate the experience should head to northern California to negotiate the **American River** located near the town of **Placerville.**

The scenes in the Indian village were shot near the city of **Kandy, Sri Lanka,** at the Hantane Tea Estate. The village, including twenty clay houses, was constructed from scratch.

The boy ruler, His Supreme Highness, guardian of Pankot tradition—the Maharajah of Pankot, Zalim Singh—lives in a magnificent palace, which was originally going to be filmed on location in India at the **Pink City of Jaipur,** but red tape intervened. Indian officials wanted so many changes to the script that it proved untenable, forcing Spielberg to reconstruct the palace at the massive **Elstree Studios** in London, where many scenes from *Star Wars* were shot.

The island of **Sri Lanka** off the coast of southern India is where the harrowing rope bridge sequence was shot, where Indy battles Mola Ram to the death. According to the script, the gorge is supposed to be three hundred feet deep, which is approximately the depth of the one used in the actual filming. (The close-ups were filmed at **Elstree Studios.**)

INDIANA JONES AND THE LAST CRUSADE

The opening scene was shot in the **Arches National Park** near Moab, Utah. The park, according to the U.S. National Park Service, features "over 2,000 natural sandstone arches, like the world-famous Delicate Arch, as well as many other unusual rock formations. In some areas, the forces of nature have millions of years of geologic history."

In the chase scene that follows, with an old-fashioned circus train chugging away, keen-eyed viewers noticed that the terrain suddenly changes from desert (the Arches National Park in Utah) to grasslands as the terrain turns hilly. It turns out that Indy's riding the **Cumbres and Toltec Scenic Railway** near the Colorado and New Mexico border, which is "hidden away in a little-known corner of the southern Rocky Mountains . . . a precious historic artifact of the American West that time forgot. Built in 1880 and little-changed since, the Cumbres and Toltec Scenic Railroad is the finest and most spectacular example of steam era mountain railroading in North America."

The Royal Masonic School in Hertfordshire, England, is where the classroom scenes of a Barnett lecture hall were shot. It also served for shots of Barnett College. (Indy taught here after teaching at Marshall College.)

The **Venice, Italy,** shots were filmed on location. This is where Indy and Dr. Marcus Brody meet Dr. Schneider, whom they had mistakenly assumed was a middle-aged male professor. (She turns out to be a tall, beautiful blonde who immediately catches Indy's eye, but he later has a change of heart. Women!)

The Church of San Barnaba, also in Venice, is where the exterior of the library was shot. This is where X marks the spot, and where Indy uses a heavy metal library rope-stand to break through the flooring to reach the catacombs beneath.

A static display of an encampment with artifacts prepared for shipment.
(Indiana Jones Stunt Spectacular, Walt Disney World, Orlando, Florida)

When Elsa Schneider announces that they've arrived at the library, Indy says, "That doesn't look much like a library." And Brody adds, "It looks like a converted church," which, in fact, it actually is. (The interior scenes, however, were *not* shot inside the church; they were shot at England's **Elstree Studios**.)

You probably remember the romantic scene at an apartment in Venice when Indy and Elsa kiss; soon afterward, it appears the apartment is ransacked. You can, if you wish, check into this room at the **Danieli Hotel** in Venice, Italy. A luxury, five-star hotel, "The Hotel Danieli is a masterfully restored palace synonymous with the splendor and romance of Venice. Only steps away from the Piazza San Marco, and legendary sites such as the Basilica, the Doge's Palace and the Bridge of Sighs," the hotel's main building "is the original fourteenth century palace of Dodge Dandolo, a Venetian gothic landmark lavishly appointed with pink marble, stained glass, gold leaf columns, Murano glass chandeliers and antiques."

Just before he's swallowed up by the flames, Indy manages to pull himself to safety.
(Indiana Jones Stunt Spectacular, Walt Disney World, Orlando, Florida)

This medieval painting was first seen in the home of Henry Jones Sr., who studied the Holy Grail legend and collected associated artifacts and artwork. (Prop replica by Anthony Magnoli)

Room rates vary significantly, depending on what room you occupy and the corresponding view. In October, for instance, a single room is 368 Euros, but a suite with lagoon view is 2,470 Euros.

Certainly, one of the most riveting chase sequences in any of the Indy films is the river chase, in which Indy and Elsa are up against members of a mysterious religious group, the Brotherhood of the Cruciform Sword. They try to kill Indy because they mistakenly assume he's out to get the Holy Grail for selfish ends, when, in fact, Indy's merely looking for his father. At the conclusion of the chase, the Turkish man, Kazim, gives them his blessings and reveals where Indy's father is being held captive.

Indy is told that his father is being held "in the Castle of Brunwald on the Austrian-German border." Although there is no lack of castles in Germany to film, the one chosen is actually in **Mayen,** which is located northwest of Frankfurt, Germany. It's actually nearer to the border with France than to Austria, which lies southeast. (The interior shots were filmed at **Elstree Studios.**)

After the movie was filmed, Spielberg felt it needed another action scene, so they filmed an exciting chase sequence in Germany; Indy and his father are on a motorcycle with a sidecar being pursued by five Nazis on motorcycles. But Germany was a little too far to go to reshoot the scene, so they used nearby Marin County in California, at the **Mt. Tamalpais State Park,** which is "just north of San Francisco and the Golden Gate . . . 6,300 acres of redwood groves, oak woodlands, grassland slopes, chaparral and rocky ridges. Offering spectacular views of the nearby Pacific and the surrounding San Francisco Bay Area, from its ridges, slopes and the 2,571-foot high East Peak."

Remember the famous Nazi Rally in Berlin? It's where books were enthusiastically burned and marching Nazis preceded their Fuhrer, whom Indy meets in a most unexpected way. If you want to take a gander at the Indy location, avoid the Motherland and get thee hence to **Buckingham, England,** to **Stowe School,** an independent coed boarding school "in the heart of the English countryside." According to its current headmaster, Dr. Anthony Wallersteiner, Stowe is "a school of unsurpassed beauty" and "embodies the ideals of the English Enlightenment. It is justifiably acclaimed for its tolerance of diversity and commitment to the pursuit of intellectual, cultural and sporting excellence." A far cry indeed from the book-burning Nazis, wouldn't you say?

When Indy and his father escape from Berlin, they do so from the Berlin Flughafen (an airport), which is where they board a zeppelin. The front of the airport with its unique, curved design cannot be found in Berlin, however. To see it, you have to travel to California, specifically, to **Treasure Island,** which is located in the San Francisco Bay between the city and Oakland. The building is at the corner of Avenue of Palms and California

Avenue. The island is accessible by car via the Bay Bridge. (The interior shots of the Berlin Flughafen and the shots of the zeppelin were filmed at **Elstree Studios.**)

It's not an Indy Jones movie unless there are multiple chase scenes. And for pure action-adventure, you can't beat the extended chase sequence in which the Nazis are in hot pursuit of Indy and his father after the pair escape in the biplane they detach from the zeppelin.

The ground scenery, though, is not Germany; it's **Mojacar, Spain,** which is, according to indigoguide.com, "located in the Spanish region of Almería on the Costa Calida. This beautiful Moorish town looks from a distance as if it might have been created from a snowfall of sugar lumps. It has a distinctly fairytale quality with its clusters of ancient whitewashed buildings clinging to the sides of the hilltop. Sandwiched between the mountains of the Sierra Cabrera and the crystal clear waters of the Mediterranean, Mojacar is the largest and most popular tourist centre of this southeastern corner of Spain."

Travelers searching for Iskenderun in the Republic of Hatay, the place in which Dr. Brody is lost at a train station and encounters the Egyptian guide Sallah, may assume that the actual film location is the city of Iskenderun in Turkey. This would be a reasonable assumption. But in fact, you have to go to Granada, Spain, to **Guadix Station,** if you want to see where it was really filmed.

By far the most imposing, magnificent structure filmed in *The Last Crusade* is the facade of the Grail temple that Indy and company reach by traveling on horseback through the Canyon of the Crescent Moon. In truth, the actual location is in the mountains of southwest Jordan at **Al Khazneh** in the ancient city of Petra.

But don't go looking for cavernous rooms, booby-trapped passageways, or a camouflaged bridge that spans two cliffs, leading to a small room where the Grail cup is safely hidden. According to Dr. Eric H. Cline, who has visited the site, you must ride horses to get through the towering canyons before reaching Petra, and once you walk beneath its towering pillars at the entrance to go inside, its interior is about the size of a small room!

And, no, there's no room with a "Great Seal." It's pure Hollywood invention built on a sound stage in **Elstree Studios** in London.

What was intended as the last Indiana Jones film had to end in a signature shot that showed everybody riding off into the sunset, which is exactly how this third movie ends. But it wasn't shot in faraway Jordan. It was shot in **Amarillo, Texas.**

A cobwebbed serpent's head commands attention from the passersby who line up to ride the jungle transports through the "Temple of the Forbidden Eye." (Indiana Jones Adventure—"The Eye of Mara," Disneyland, Anaheim, California)

PART 5

Archaeology

"FOR MANY YEARS, THE STEREOTYPICAL ARCHAEOLOGIST, AS PORTRAYED BY ACTORS, WORE A UNIFORM OF PITH HELMET, KNEE SOCKS, KHAKI SHORTS, AND SAFARI JACKET, WHILE HE SUPERVISED NATIVES DIGGING IN THE SANDS OF NEAR EASTERN DESERTS. INDIANA JONES ADDED OTHER DIMENSIONS TO THIS STEREOTYPE, ONES THAT ARE JUST AS MISLEADING AS THOSE THAT CAME BEFORE HIS PORTRAYAL. ARCHAEOLOGISTS ARE NO MORE LIKELY TO BECOME INVOLVED IN WILD, HAIR-RAISING ADVENTURES THAN AN AVERAGE TOURIST."

—Bill McMillon, *The Archaeology Handbook:*
A Field Manual and Resource Guide

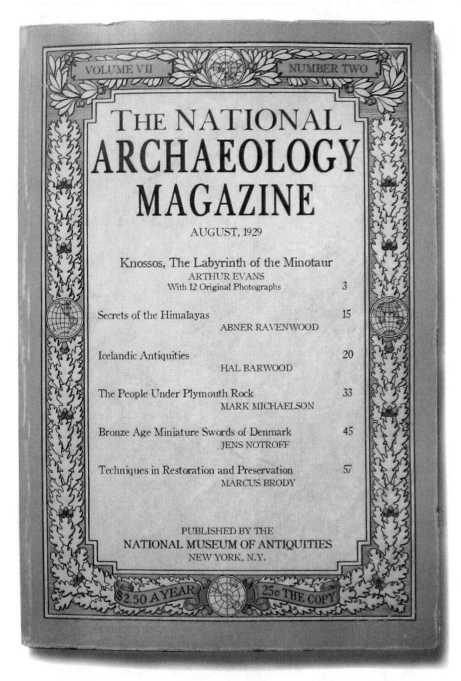

VOLUME VII   NUMBER TWO

THE NATIONAL
ARCHAEOLOGY
MAGAZINE

AUGUST, 1929

Knossos, The Labyrinth of the Minotaur
ARTHUR EVANS
With 12 Original Photographs   3

Secrets of the Himalayas   15
ABNER RAVENWOOD

Icelandic Antiquities   20
HAL BARWOOD

The People Under Plymouth Rock   33
MARK MICHAELSON

Bronze Age Miniature Swords of Denmark   45
JENS NOTROFF

Techniques in Restoration and Preservation   57
MARCUS BRODY

PUBLISHED BY THE
NATIONAL MUSEUM OF ANTIQUITIES
NEW YORK, N.Y.

$2.50 A YEAR   25c THE COPY

An issue of *The National Archaeology Magazine,* whose contributors include
Abner Ravenwood and Marcus Brody. (Prop replica by Anthony Magnoli)

FIELD NOTES ON ARCHAEOLOGY

In the wake of the success of the Indiana Jones movie franchise, we've seen Angelina Jolie in *Lara Croft: Tomb Raider* and *Lara Croft, Tomb Raider: The Cradle of Life;* Brendan Fraser in *The Mummy* and *The Mummy Returns;* and a host of other adventure-oriented films that give the erroneous impression that archaeologists live a life of thrills, chills, and spills—alas, it's all Hollywood fiction.

In real life, archaeology has little to do with the art of making movies and everything to do with artifacts: physical proof of former civilizations in the form of relics left behind, which give us tantalizing clues to how they lived.

The *Encyclopedia Britannica* online states:

Archaeology is the scientific study of the material remains of past human life and activities. These include human artifacts from the very earliest stone tools to the man-made objects that are buried or thrown away in the present day: everything made by human beings—from simple tools to complex machines, from the earliest houses and temples and tombs to the palaces, cathedrals, and pyramids. Archaeological investigations are a principal source of knowledge of prehistoric, ancient, and extinct culture. . . . The archaeologist is first a descriptive worker: he has to describe, classify, and analyze the artifacts he studies. An adequate and objective taxonomy is the basis of all archaeology, and many good archaeologists spend their lives in this activity of description and classification. But the main aim of the archaeologist is to place the material remains in historical contexts, to supplement what may be known from written sources, and, thus, to increase understanding of the past. Ultimately, then, the archaeologist is a historian: his aim is the interpretive description of the past of man.

A thorough discussion of archaeology—what it does, how a site is prepared, how a dig proceeds, the technological advances that have substantially changed the field in the last few years—would be a book in itself, and a large book at that. Moreover, on this subject, you are well advised to get expert advice instead of a layman's, which is why I'm pleased to republish what I think is an important essay by Dr. Eric H. Cline, who wears two hats: in the classroom, he's a professor of archaeology at George Washington University in Washington, D.C.; and out on a dig, he's a working field archaeologist.

Dr. Cline's article herein, "Raiders of the Faux Ark," explains thoroughly the big difference between the tomb raiders who prey on an unsuspecting public and the legitimate work done by archaeologists with bona fide credentials. As you will see, it's a world of difference.

Clearly someone has been waiting in line too long. (Indiana Jones Adventure—"The Eye of Mara," Disneyland, Anaheim, California)

Following his article is "Digging It: A Day in the Life of a Field Archaeologist." Most people (including myself) have never been on a dig and have no idea what a typical day in the field is like. Here, Dr. Cline, who has been on countless digs all over the world, describes it for us.

Finally, I've appended an article that talks about some of the legitimate and fabled places and artifacts that have fascinated (and frustrated) amateurs and professionals alike.

Then it's time for me to take you back to the classroom, so to speak, and let you know what other resources are available for self-study, so you can do a little digging on your own.

The treasure map used by Indy in the opening scenes
of the first movie. (Prop replica by Anthony Magnoli)

A wooden-faced statue greets guests who enter Adventureland. (Magic Kingdom, Walt Disney World, Orlando, Florida)

RAIDERS OF THE FAUX ARK

by Dr. Eric H. Cline

Noah's Ark. The Ark of the Covenant. The Garden of Eden. Sodom and Gomorrah. The Exodus. The Lost Tomb of Jesus. All have been "found" in the last ten years, including one within the past six months. The discoverers: a former SWAT team member; an investigator of ghosts, telepathy, and parapsychology; a filmmaker who calls himself "The Naked Archaeologist"; and others, none of whom has any professional training in archaeology.

We are living in a time of exciting discoveries in biblical archaeology. We are also living in a time of widespread biblical fraud, dubious science, and crackpot theorizing. Some of the highest-profile discoveries of the past several years are shadowed by accusations of forgery, such as the James Ossuary, which may or may not be the burial box of Jesus' brother, as well as other supposed Bible-era findings such as the Jehoash Tablet and a small ivory pomegranate said to be from the time of Solomon. Every year "scientific" expeditions embark to look for Noah's Ark, raising untold amounts of money from gullible believers who eagerly listen to tales spun by sincere amateurs or rapacious con men; it is not always easy to tell the two apart.

The tools of modern archaeology, from magnetometers to precise excavation methods, offer a growing opportunity to illuminate some of the intriguing mysteries surrounding the Bible, one of the foundations of western civilization. Yet the amateurs are taking the public's money to support ventures that offer little chance of furthering the cause of knowledge. With their grand claims, and all the ensuing attention, they divert the public's attention from the scientific study of the Holy Land—and bring confusion, and even discredit, to biblical archaeology.

Unfortunately, when fantastic claims are made, they go largely unchallenged by academics. There have been some obvious exceptions, such as

Indy and Marion hide out behind a fifty-gallon oil drum in this "filmed" reenactment. (Indiana Jones Stunt Spectacular, Walt Disney World, Orlando, Florida)

the recent film *The Lost Tomb of Jesus,* which inspired an outcry from scholars in response to its claim that archaeologists had found, but not recognized, the tomb of Jesus more than twenty years ago. But much more common is a vast and echoing silence reminiscent of the early days of the debate over "intelligent design," when biologists were reluctant to respond to the neocreationist challenge. Archaeologists, too, are often reluctant to be seen as challenging deeply held religious beliefs. And so the professionals are allowing a public relations disaster to unfold: yielding a field of tremendous importance to pseudo scientists, amateur enthusiasts, and irresponsible documentary filmmakers.

At a time when the world is increasingly divided by religion, both domestically and internationally, and when many people are biblically illiterate, legitimate inquiries into the common origins of religions have never been more important. I believe that the public deserves—and wants—better. We have an obligation to challenge the lies and the hype, to share the real data, so that the public discussion can be an informed one.

It is time we take back our field.

The first archaeological endeavors in the Holy Land were conducted not by archaeologists, but rather by theologians primarily interested in locating places mentioned in the Bible. Among the first was American minister Edward Robinson, who toured the Holy Land in 1838, accompanied by an American missionary named Eli Smith who was fluent in Arabic. Their goal was to identify as many sites mentioned in the Bible as possible, in other words, to create a historical (and biblical) geography of Palestine. Others soon followed, including Sir Charles Warren, a British general who explored and recorded the features of Jerusalem in the 1860s. None of these men were archaeologists, but they made important contributions to the field.

Throughout much of the nineteenth century, the field of biblical archaeology was dominated by men said to have been working with a Bible in one hand and a trowel in the other. The field soon became more scientific, thanks to the efforts of men like Sir William Matthew Flinders Petrie, who introduced into archaeology the dual concepts of stratigraphy (when two succeeding cities are built one on top of the other, the lower one will always be earlier in time) and pottery seriation (pottery types go in and out of style, just like today's clothes, and can be used to help date the stratigraphic levels observable at ancient sites).

By the time Dame Kathleen Kenyon was excavating in Jericho and Jerusalem in the mid-twentieth century, archaeology was in the hands of professionals trained not just in proper excavation techniques, but in the scientific method, and with years of schooling in ancient languages, cultures, and history. They also mastered bodies of literature and theory and spent years practicing their craft and being subjected to peer review. Theological motivation became less important.

This bag of gold coins was given to Indy in payment for an urn
supposedly containing the remains of Chinese emperor Nurhache
in the second movie. (Prop replica by Anthony Magnoli)

Today there are strict standards concerning excavations in every country in the Middle East. Permission to excavate must be obtained from the proper authorities, with presentation of a detailed research plan, good reasons given for the questions being examined, evidence of sufficient funding, and often a strategy for conservation of the site upon completion of the excavation. Peer review of any large funding proposals is obligatory. In short, it is a serious and highly competitive field.

As a result, however, we have seen a rise of two cultures—the scientists and the amateur enthusiasts. Lacking the proper training and credentials, the amateurs are sustained by vanity presses, television, and now the Internet.

For example, in 2006, Bob Cornuke, a former SWAT team member turned biblical investigator—and now president of the Bible Archaeology Search and Exploration (BASE) Institute in Colorado—led an expedition searching for Noah's Ark. Media reports breathlessly announced that Cornuke's team had discovered boat-shaped rocks at an altitude of 13,000 feet on Mount Suleiman in Iran's Elburz mountain range. Cornuke said the rocks look "uncannily like wood. . . . We have had thin sections of the rock made [cut], and we can see [wood] cell structures."

But peer review would have quickly debunked these findings. Kevin Pickering, a geologist at University College London who specializes in sedimentary rocks, said, "The photos appear to show iron-stained sedimentary rocks, probably thin beds of silicified sandstones and shales, which were most likely laid down in a marine environment a long time ago."

Then there is Michael Sanders, who has made a habit of using NASA satellite photographs to search for biblical locations and objects. From 1998 to 2001, Sanders made announcements that he had located the lost cities of Sodom and Gomorrah, the Garden of Eden, the Ark of the Covenant, and the Tower of Babel.

Sanders describes himself on his website as a "Biblical Scholar of Archaeology, Egyptology and Assyriology," but according to the *Los Angeles Times,* he "concedes that he has no formal archaeological training." Other newspaper accounts describe him as a "self-made scholar" who did research in parapsychology at Duke University.

And we must not forget documentary filmmaker Simcha Jacobovici.

He bills himself as "The Naked Archaeologist" in a television series on the History Channel, but has repeatedly stated during media interviews that he is an investigative journalist rather than an archaeologist. Jacobovici is perhaps best known for *The Lost Tomb of Jesus,* which first aired in March 2007 and which has been described by professor Jodi Magness of the University of North Carolina at Chapel Hill as making "a sensationalistic claim without any scientific basis or support."

In short, the amateur arena is full of deeply flawed junk science. Important issues are cloaked in legitimate-sounding terminology, little attention is paid to the investigative process, and contrary evidence is ignored.

Biblical archaeologists are suddenly finding themselves in a position similar to the evolutionary biologists fighting intelligent design: An entire parallel version of their field is being driven by religious belief, not research principles. The biologists' situation makes the risk clear; they did not deign to mount a public refutation of the "science" of intelligent design for years, until it was almost too late, and thus antievolutionary science began making its way into the public schools.

Why are we sitting the battle out?

Partly, this is a matter of a strain of snobbery that runs through many academic fields: a suspicion of colleagues who venture too far from "serious" topics or appear in the popular media too often.

Partly it is a matter of the uncertainty of the stories themselves: Many biblical questions are so shrouded in uncertainty as to be inherently unsolvable. For example, even if the Garden of Eden were a real place, and even if we knew the general location where it might have been, how would we know when we found it? When most archaeologists and biblical scholars hear that someone has (yet again) discovered Noah's Ark, they roll their eyes and get on with their business. This can leave the impression that the report might be true.

And partly it is because scientific findings may challenge religious dogma. Biblical scholarship is highly charged because the Bible is a religious book and any research carries the prospect of "proving" or "disproving" treasured beliefs. What if the Exodus might not have taken place as described in the Bible? Similarly, what will people do when told that there are identical stories to Noah and the Ark, but they were recorded between five hundred and one thousand years earlier sans Noah? And that the flood was sent because the people were too noisy and the Gods couldn't sleep, not because people were evil and sinning? Or when you tell them that "an eye for an eye, a tooth for a tooth" was a concept expressed in Hammurabi's Law Code nearly a thousand years before the Bible?

This is where it can get daunting for academics, for it is at this point that the ideologues frequently weigh in. And these pundits are often sophisticated and convincing debaters, which can make them intimidating opponents for a scholar.

But we don't need to go looking for Noah's Ark to find confirmation of details found in the Bible. During the past century or so, archaeologists have found the first mention of Israel outside the Bible, in an Egyptian inscription carved by the Pharaoh Merneptah in the year 1207 BC. They

A sword-wielding henchman stands up to Indiana Jones in the marketplace.
(Indiana Jones Stunt Spectacular, Walt Disney World, Orlando, Florida)

133

have found mentions of Israelite kings, including Omri, Ahab, and Jehu, in neo-Assyrian inscriptions from the early first millennium BC. And they have found, most recently, a mention of the House of David in an inscription from northern Israel dating to the ninth century BC. These are conclusive pieces of evidence that these people and places once existed and that at least parts of the Bible are historically accurate. Perhaps none of these is as attention-getting as finding Noah's Ark, but they serve to deepen our understanding of, and appreciation for, the Bible.

Religious archaeologists and secular archaeologists frequently work side by side in the Holy Land. Among the top ranks of researchers, there are evangelical Christians, orthodox Jews, and people of many denominations. It is not religious views that are the issue here; it is whether good science is being done. Biblical archaeology is a field in which people of good will, and all religions, can join under the banner of the scientific process.

Most archaeological organizations, including the American Schools of Oriental Research, the Archaeological Institute of America, and the Society for American Archaeology, state that it is one of the obligations of professional archaeologists to make their findings and discoveries generally available. But we need to do more than simply publish research if we are to successfully counter junk science. We need to take our information to the public not only via writing but also via radio, television, film, and any other available media.

Remember that biblical mysteries are not just ancient history. For example, did Joshua really fight the Battle of Jericho and drive the Canaanites out of the land, as stated in the biblical account of the Israelite conquest of Canaan? If so, who was there first and to whom does the land really belong today? Does it matter? It does to many Palestinians, who exert a claim as descendants of the Canaanites and Jebusites, and to many Israelis, who exert a similar claim based on their own understanding of their ancestors' history.

Remember, too, that archaeologists who speak out can make a difference. "Disclaimer statements" have recently been posted on Bob Cornuke's Web pages concerning the Ark of the Covenant, Noah's Ark, and the location of Mount Sinai. Now, for instance, we find the statement that the BASE Institute "does not make the claim that we have found Noah's Ark. We'll let you draw your own conclusions. In our opinion, it's a candidate. The research continues."

Even when our own investigations come up empty—we can't solve all the mysteries in the Bible—we can present the current state of our evidence. And we can promote a shared methodology, and a shared body of facts, that can be used by everyone. The data and opinions that we provide may not end any debates, but they will introduce genuine archaeological and historical data and considerations into the mix. We owe it to the ancient world, and to the people who inhabited it, to do no less.

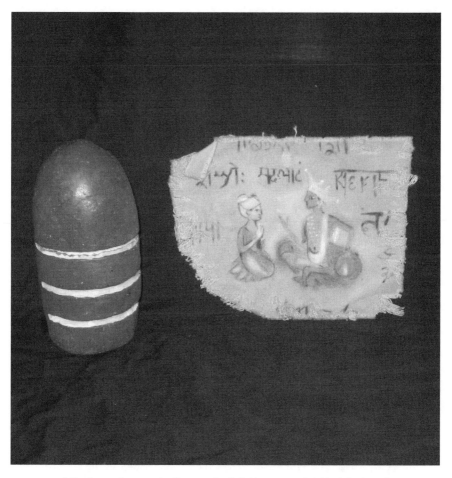

A Sankara stone and a fragment of cloth manuscript that featured prominently in the second movie. (Prop replicas by Anthony Magnoli)

NOTE: This piece originally appeared in the *Boston Globe* (September 30, 2007) and is reprinted with the permission of its author, Dr. Eric H. Cline, who is the author (among other books) of *From Eden to Exile: Unraveling Mysteries of the Bible.* He is chair of the department of classical and Semitic languages and literature at George Washington University in Washington, D.C. He is also associate director (USA) of the ongoing excavations at Megiddo (biblical Armageddon) in Israel. His website is at http://home.gwu.edu/~ehcline/.

DIGGING IT: A DAY IN THE LIFE OF A FIELD ARCHAEOLOGIST

If you've seen the Indiana Jones movies, you probably think a typical field day for an archaeologist is when you get chased by the indigenous population, meet nefarious enemies, encounter beautiful women who need rescuing, negotiate otherwise impossible obstacles, recover priceless antiquities, and miraculously manage to do all with nary a scratch and your skin wholly intact.

Well, that's the Hollywood version.

What's a *real* day like in the life of a field archaeologist?

A veteran of "twenty-three seasons of archaeological excavation and surveys in Israel, Egypt, Jordan, Greece, Cypress, and the USA," Dr. Eric Cline is equally comfortable in and out of the classroom: A professor and a field archaeologist, he finds the Indiana Jones movies great fun to watch and says he will be the first in line, with his family in tow, to see the fourth movie. He readily acknowledges, however, that there's usually just a grain of truth in the movies, whereas in real life, archaeology is a painstaking, time-consuming, thoroughly documented process. Sifting through grains of ancient soil is often a matter of many years of labor, involving meticulous work by a small army of people who must function as a team to carefully document and chronicle by all available means (video, digital photography, written notes) all findings from initial discovery through excavation and laboratory work to eventual publication.

Clearly, in a field that calls for taking infinite pains from start to finish, the average day in the life of an archaeologist on site is prosaic and filled with routine—at least in comparison to Indiana Jones's adventures. But the joy of uncovering artifacts from bygone civilizations brings its own thrill of recognition, of discovery, with the goal of sharing the findings with

VANITY FAIR

NO. 570

*"Indiana Jones!
I always knew some day
you'd come walking
back through my door."
— MARION RAVENWOOD
(KAREN ALLEN) IN RAIDERS
OF THE LOST ARK.*

EXCLUSIVE!
2008
FIRST LOOK!

INDY'S BACK!

(And Guess Who's Riding Shotgun!)

HARRISON FORD, STEVEN SPIELBERG, GEORGE LUCAS, AND SHIA LaBEOUF

Spill the Beans on the 15-Years-in-the-Making Sequel

BY JIM WINDOLF • PHOTOS BY ANNIE LEIBOVITZ

INTRIGUES:
NSIGHTS ON
'S DEATH
BLACKMAIL PLOT
MINICK DUNNE

FEBRUARY 2008/$4.95 U.S
WWW.VANITYFAIR.CO

02>
08443
0 751164 6

The cover to *Vanity Fair* (February 2008) with Shia LaBeouf and Harrison Ford on the set. The issue contained a lengthy article, "Keys to the Kingdom," by Jim Windolf, and photographs by Annie Leibowitz. The magazine supplemented its print coverage with two interviews (George Lucas and Steven Spielberg) that were exclusive to the website.

the world at large and gaining a deeper understanding and appreciation of past civilizations.

To know our past is to understand our present and give us a glimpse of our future, so archaeologists are in effect mining for information that helps us understand who we are as people.

Recalling the summers he's spent at a dig in Megiddo, Israel, Dr. Cline explains what constitutes his normal day.

As is obvious to anyone who has traveled to the Middle East, its summer climate is ideal for digging. According to the *CIA World Factbook,* "Israel has a Mediterranean climate characterized by long, hot, dry summers" and, from June to August, it's "often rainless." So the principal concern is the heat, which reaches its peak in August, when the temperature can climb to over a hundred degrees.

Though diggers work in the shade, the usual uniform is utilitarian: loose-fitting short-sleeved shirt, short pants, headgear (often a baseball cap, not a pith helmet!), sunglasses, and plenty of water to prevent dehydration.

Though one does become acclimated, the fact remains that it's important to be in good physical shape because a day's work will take its toll.

The core staff consists of an experienced crew: two directors, an associate director (in this case, Dr. Cline), a bone specialist, a camp manager responsible for logistics, and an office manager. The students, working for college credits, act as diggers.

At the Megiddo dig, the site is laid out in six designated areas. Each area, which has five to twenty "squares," has a supervisor assigned, who oversees all activities. Working under the supervisors are the "square" supervisors, who work with the diggers, the volunteers whose ranks include people from different countries and all walks of life, though most are college students. The diggers do the grunt work, the time-consuming, exacting work of using small hand tools to excavate pottery.

Keeping in mind the necessity to document each find in situ, a photographer is on hand with a digital camera to record artifacts as they are found. A black placard is used to record all relevant data. Then each piece must then be taken to a location for careful washing.

Additionally, a person acting as a recorder (a scribe, if you will) supplements the photographic record with textual notes.

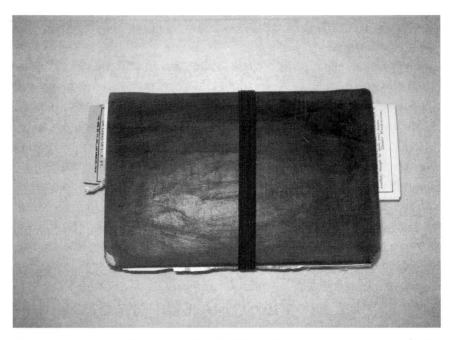

The banded exterior of Henry Jones Sr.'s Grail Diary. (Prop replica by Anthony Magnoli)

The interior of Henry Jones Sr.'s Grail Diary showing the knight's tomb in a stained-glass window in Venice. (Prop replica by Anthony Magnoli)

On any given day, buckets of pieces of broken, dirty pottery—usually excavated in pieces, not intact—require careful handling to remove hundreds of years of encrustation from each piece. After brushing with a small hand whisk and carefully washing the piece, the pottery is set out to dry, so that the next day specialists can assist in properly identifying the piece—"reading" it, as Dr. Cline explains, to establish its date. Like clothing, pottery "fashions" go in and out of style. The style can last for months, years, and sometimes decades, so the style of the pottery itself—determined by looking at its rim, its handle, or other distinctive features—is a key indicator for dating purposes.

Typically, the workweek consists of five days, with weekends reserved for private time; because of the heat, the day for supervisors and diggers necessarily starts, and ends, early.

4:00 a.m. Get up and get dressed. Maybe grab a quick cup of coffee, but a normal breakfast will have to wait. Get organized for the day, get your tools out, and travel by bus to the site and get to your designated square.

5:00 a.m. It's sunrise and time to start digging. You'll be digging for a few hours. There's a covered canopy, but you'll still be hot and, as the day wears on, thirsty. (Bring bottled water.)

8:00 to 9:00 a.m. Time to break for breakfast. It's usually a half-hour, a catered breakfast served on site, not at a sit-down cafeteria or eatery back at the kibbutz.

9:00 to 11:00 a.m. More digging.

11:00 a.m. A fifteen-minute water break.

11:15 a.m. to 12:30 p.m. More digging. Then the digging stops. That's it for the day. You get back on the bus and head back to the kibbutz where a catered lunch has been prepared.

1:00 to 4:00 p.m. Lunchtime immediately followed by private time. Most people either take a well-deserved (and needed) nap, though the more energetic souls (the college students) often prefer physical recreational activities: soccer, basketball, or swimming at the pool (always a welcome relief from the unrelenting summer heat).

4:00 to 6:00 p.m. This is when all the hard work pays off. It's time to carefully wash the pottery and have the specialists do the identification. (The pottery will later to sent to a laboratory for further analysis, depending on what is found.)

A medieval painting seen in the house of Henry Jones Sr.,
who collects Grail memorabilia. (Prop replica by Anthony Magnoli)

7:00 p.m. Dinnertime.

8:00 to 9:00 p.m. Classes are held on pertinent subjects: introduction
to the history of archaeology, ancient Israel, introduction to field techniques and methodology. For graduate students, a separate class is usually
held; one of the topics might be "From artifacts to texts and beyond." In
other words, there's something for everyone.

Keeping in mind that wake-up call is only seven hours away, the wiser
heads usually opt for calling it a night, but typically the college students
still have energy to burn and often hang out with their peers and talk, play
musical instruments, sing, and otherwise decompress from a long day.

Then, at 4:00 a.m., the day starts up again for everyone.

The weekends are a welcome break, allowing people to travel.
Sometimes formal field trips are arranged, but often the excursions are
informal and organized in small groups by people with shared interests.

One piece of pottery, two pieces, many pieces . . . and from them, over a period of time—months, certainly years—the archaeologists on site will piece together the story of an ancient race that, like us, enjoyed their day in the sun and left behind the artifacts of their lives for future generations to uncover and discover human history.

The interior of young Indiana Jones's passport; it traces Indy's adventures until his enlistment in the Belgian army. (Prop replica by Anthony Magnoli)

Curiously conjoined, this smiling statue welcomes guests to Adventureland. (Magic Kingdom, Walt Disney World, Orlando, Florida)

FABLED PLACES AND RELICS, LOST CITIES, AND ANCIENT CIVILIZATIONS

Although it's true that, as an archaeologist (or amateur adventurer-traveler, for that matter), you aren't likely to get chased by Indians through a rain forest, find yourself in the clutches of tall, leggy blondes with dastardly deeds in mind, or have a shoot-out with Nazis in a Tibetan bar, there are still archaeological worlds to see, to conquer, now shrouded in the dim mists of antiquity.

Archaeology is, after all, the study of the artifacts that humankind has left behind, so these mysterious places raise more questions than can be answered. The following are some truly unique places around the world that hint at ancient civilizations replete with mysteries.

Given that Indiana Jones has searched for the Lost Ark of the Covenant, ancient Indian stones, the Holy Grail, and a priceless Crystal Skull reputed to have otherworldly powers, where might Dr. Jones be found next? Keep in mind that we're going to be all over the map (so to speak) and talk about legitimate as well as fabled sites.

Here are some likely candidates:

ATLANTIS

There's no question that among lost worlds, none so irresistibly and tantalizingly commands attention as the Lost City of Atlantis. Supposedly sited (if Plato is correct) beyond the Straits of Gibraltar, the inhabitants of this lost city—like those from Sodom and Gomorrah—were wicked and the city sank into the ocean. (For more information, check out Plato's *Timaeus* and *Critias*.)

Over the years, many have searched in vain for Atlantis, hoping to find the remains of a fabled lost city, but it remains elusive. Despite the advances in deep-sea exploration, no evidence has turned up that suggests Atlantis actually existed.

If Atlantis is out there, somewhere, it's obviously submerged and likely well preserved: artifacts of every kind, rare coins and jewels, and other valuable items could be there, waiting for an adventurous, deep-seagoing archaeologist.

But take these tales of Atlantis with a grain—no, a pound—of salt.

Actually, if you want to visit Atlantis, it *does* exist and can be found in

the Bahamas, at Paradise Island. It's a beautiful resort, though, not a fabled city that rose from beneath the waves. Its website is www.atlantis.com.

EASTER ISLAND

Location: 2,200 miles west of Chile (South America)
Date: unknown
Also called Rapa Nui, this island in the middle of nowhere is home to three-story stone statues that number in the hundreds.

Who built them and why were they built? What happened to the indigenous population that once numbered an estimated tens of thousands on this remote island in the Pacific that measures a scant sixty-five miles? Were they struck by an ecological disaster? A man-made catastrophe?

When the island was "discovered" in 1722 on Easter (hence its name, Easter Island), the isolated population numbered two thousand and, not surprisingly, they were astonished to discover that they were not alone in the world.

Unanswered questions remain: How were these eighty-ton statues moved from quarry to sites for erection? We can only speculate.

GREAT PYRAMID

Location: Near Cairo, Egypt
Date: Built from 2750 BC to 1300 AD
Anyone with any interest in archaeology is fascinated by the Great Pyramid at Giza (or al-Jizah, as it was called in the days of the fourth dynasty of Egypt). What's amazing about the Pyramid of Khufu, the Great Pyramid, is its size and precision of construction. The *Encyclopedia Britannica* notes that "The simple measurements of the Great Pyramid indicate very adequately its scale, monumentality, and precision: its sides are 755.43 feet, 756.08 feet, 755.88 feet, and 755.77 feet. Its height is 481.4 feet."

Built as a funerary for Egyptian kings, this housed King Khufu, whose mummified body and gold treasure have never been found. So, one asks, where is the treasure? And, just as important, where is King Khufu? No one knows. Another mystery. Lost, no doubt, in the shifting sands of time.

▲

THE HOLY LANCE

Like the Holy Grail, the Holy Lance's connection to history is Christ, who, on the cross, was pierced by the lance of a Roman soldier.

The Holy Lance, then, became the stuff of history as it supposedly changed hands among military leaders beginning with a Roman emperor, Constantine the Great.

The legend surrounding the Holy Lance is that, like the Ark of the Covenant, its power is such that none can stand before it. So he who wields the Lance holds divine power in his hands and, thus, could conquer the world.

But that's more myth than fact. Though the original owner of the Holy Lance claimed he saw its location—in the Cathedral of St. Peter—in a vision, historians are dubious.

Similarly, as for the claims that Hitler was actively hunting for the Holy Lance, no factual evidence supports it. (For a somewhat fanciful account of this artifact, read Trevor Ravenscroft's book *The Spear of Destiny*.)

KING TUTANKHAMEN'S TOMB

Location: Egypt

Date: Early 1300s BC

Discovered by British archaeologist Howard Carter during a dig in 1922, King Tut's tomb had lain undisturbed for centuries. Carter describes what he discovered: "It was some time before one could see, the hot air escaping caused the candle to flicker, but as soon as one's eyes became accustomed to the glimmer of light the interior of the chamber gradually loomed before one, with its strange and wonderful medley of extraordinary and beautiful objects heaped upon one another." It took a decade just to remove the contents of this treasure trove.

The one Egyptian king most people can name is King Tut, owing to the rotating exhibit of 130 artifacts that traveled worldwide, drawing millions of curious viewers. (Comedian Steve Martin also raised public awareness with his stand-up routine, "A Tribute to King Tut.")

NAZCA LINES

Location: northwest of Nazca in southern Peru (South America)

Date: 200 BC to 600 AD

It's said that if you've only seen Earth from ground level, you haven't seen Earth at all. In discussing the Nazca Lines, this is certainly true because you can only see them from the bird's point of view.

Comprising hundreds of precise geometric shapes (geoglyphs) and seventy images of flora and fauna (biomorphs), these intriguing symbols have given rise to numerous speculations, including that an ancient civilization from another world used this site for an extraterrestrial landing zone. You know what I'm talking about: little green men and flying saucers. We are not alone in the universe . . . or *are* we?

It's worth a gander and the price of a plane ticket just for its curiosity value. But don't go looking for extraterrestrials, who can be found in mummified form in Nevada at the top-secret air force base, Area 51.

NOAH'S ARK

Like other biblical artifacts, the Ark has never been found. Those familiar with the Bible will recall that, in Genesis (6:11–9:19), God decides that the corruption on Earth requires his divine intervention. He tells Noah, whom the Lord considered a righteous man, to construct an ark and take aboard all the world's species of animals with which to replenish the population. Noah's three sons (Shem, Ham, and Japheth) and their wives, of course, would repopulate humankind.

Then God created the great flood and every living thing perished, except those who found sanctuary on the ark.

The mystery here is simply this: What is the location of the Ark today? Given that there was a Great Flood, might the Ark be on a mountaintop, where it rested after the waters receded? After all, it "came to rest upon the mountains of Ararat," the Bible tells us.

Interestingly, on top of Mount Ararat, there's an anomaly, an unexplained phenomenon: a large object at approximately 16,000 feet in elevation. Aerial photography substantiates the existence of something large at that altitude, but just what it is, no one knows. It's a mystery cloaked in ice over centuries, but is it the lost Ark?

Well, many want to believe so, but the scientific community has debunked this theory. That hasn't stopped some people who still maintain that it's the real deal.

Indy and Marion pole-vault to safety. (Indiana Jones
Stunt Spectacular, Walt Disney World, Orlando, Florida)

STONEHENGE

Location: Wiltshire, England

Date: 3100 BC

Not surprisingly, Stonehenge is in ruins because of unnatural and nat-ural damage. Vandals and souvenir-seekers have taken their toll on this enigmatic structure; furthermore, its exposure to the elements since the Neolithic period has significantly eroded these standing stones.

As to why it was built, no one knows for sure. As R. J. C. Atkinson (archaeologist, University College, Cardiff) explains, "Most of what has been written about Stonehenge is nonsense or speculation. No one will ever have a clue what its significance was." But that doesn't stop people from wondering, guessing, and putting forth some of the most outlandish theories imaginable.

TOWER OF BABEL

Location: city of Babylon (Iraq)

Date: predates 600 BC

Like the Lost Ark of the Covenant, the Tower of Babel has its origins in the Bible. Genesis 11:1–9 tells the story of the Babylonians who attempted to build a tower "with its top in the heavens." God, however, didn't take too kindly to this exhibition of man-made hubris and made it impossible for construction to continue when he made the workers speak different languages; thus, they were unable to communicate with one another, and work quickly ceased on this edifice—a monument, as it were, to man's colossal ego.

But does the Tower actually exist? According to archaeologists working in Babylon, a foundation of immense size, measuring three hundred feet on each of its four sides, was discovered.

Could it be the biblical Tower? Or perhaps another ancient structure with no connection to the Christian world? Or (pardon my lisp) a myth-take? Inquiring minds want to know.

An enigmatic but friendly face greets guests at Adventureland. (Magic Kingdom, Walt Disney World, Orlando, Florida)

ARCHAEOLOGICAL RESOURCES

BOOKS

There are many outstanding books on the subject of archaeology, but here are a few of my favorites. Reading these will certainly get you on the right track, and lead you to other books as well.

Archaeology, by Dr. Jane McIntosh. New York: Knopf, 1994. Hardback (paper on board), 64 pages, $25.99. Though intended for young adult readers, this is a useful and informative text for readers of all ages, because

This cloth manuscript tells a story that is at the heart of the second Indiana Jones movie. (Prop replica by Anthony Magnoli)

it's wonderfully illustrated in full color with rare photos and authoritative text. (Dr. Jane McIntosh is also the author of *Practical Archaeologist,* now in its second edition.)

The Archaeology Handbook: A Field Manual and Resource Guide, by Bill McMillon. New York: Wiley, 1991. Trade paperback, 259 pages, $26.95. I suspect the high price is because of the high cost of print-on-demand technology used to produce the book, which suffers from lackluster reproduction of photographs. Though McMillon is not an archaeologist, he certainly has dug up all the basic information about the subject and presents it to the layperson in an accessible manner. It's actually two books in one: a general introduction to archaeology, and a resource guide listing travel agencies, museums, archaeological sites, excavations, field schools, organizations that assist with the placement of volunteers, state archaeologists and state historic preservation officers, archaeological organizations, and much more. Clearly, he's done his homework, so there's no point in me being redundant and listing some of these resources when it's all in one book for your easy reference. (Note: He does *not* provide Web addresses, but does provide phone numbers and mailing addresses.)

The Atlas of Archaeology, by Mick Aston and Tim Taylor. New York: DK Books, 1998. Hardback, 208 pages. Out of print. An oversized book, this is a treasure trove of information. It's billed as "the definitive guide to the location, history and significance of the world's most important archaeological sites and finds," and it lives up to that billing. Illustrated in full color, with maps galore, this is a wonderful resource for people who want to do some exploring on their own.

MAGAZINES

American Antiquity. Published quarterly by the Society for American Archaeology (www.saa.org). According to the Society, this is "a quarterly journal devoted to the archaeology of the New World, method and theory pertinent to the study of New World archaeology, and closely related subjects."

American Journal of Archaeology. Published quarterly by the Archaeological Institute of America (www.ajaonline.org). Issues (in Adobe PDF format) may be viewed online for free. Its mandate is, according to

Naomi J. Norman, editor in chief: "to publish articles devoted to the art and archaeology of ancient Europe and the Mediterranean world, including the Near East and Egypt, from prehistoric to Late Antique times." Its audience is professionals in the field.

Archaeology. Published by the Archaeological Institute of America, this is less academic, though written by professionals in the field for a general audience. Sumptuously illustrated.

WEBSITES

The armchair traveler will find a wealth of information online, more, in fact, than you could imagine; the links alone would take days to explore. Here are some of the major sites worth your attention:

http://archnet.asu.edu is maintained by the staff at the Archaeological Research Institute at Arizona State University.

http://www.nps.gov/history is maintained by the National Park Service, U.S. Department of the Interior.

http://www.nmai.si.edu is maintained by the Smithsonian's National Museum of the American Indian.

http://www.nationaltrust.org is maintained by the National Trust for Historic Preservation.

http://ww.saa.org is maintained by the Society for American Archaeology.

http://www.sha.org is maintained by the Society for Historical Archaeology.

http://www.nps.gov/archeology is maintained by the National Park Service, U.S. Department of the Interior.

PART 6

General
Resources

Indiana Jones's instantly recognizable gear and clothing: a fedora, a bullwhip, a leather jacket, and a khaki work shirt. (Prop replicas by Anthony Magnoli)

BOOKS ABOUT INDIANA JONES

The Complete Making of Indiana Jones, by J. W. Rinzler and Laurent Bouzereau. Preface by George Lucas, foreword by Steven Spielberg. New York: Del Rey Books, 2008. Trade paperback, 288 pages, $35. A coffee-table book that focuses only on the four films, this is "a behind-the-scenes look at the people, places, technology, and events that went into the creation of all four Indiana Jones movies," according to the publisher.

From Star Wars to Indiana Jones: The Best of the Lucasfilm Archives, by Mark Cotta Vaz and Shinji Hata. San Francisco: Chronicle Books, 1994. Trade paperback, 208 pages, $22.95. Another coffee-table book that takes you into the fabled George Lucas vault to see its "incredible collection of costumes, props, puppets, models, and matte paintings . . . behind-the-scenes production illustrations, storyboards, and prototypes—many of the images published for the first time." Indy fans will love the chapters jam-packed with information about how they made the Indiana Jones films.

Sankara stones—so that's what makes them glow! (Prop replicas by Anthony Magnoli)

George Lucas: The Creative Impulse, by Charles Champlin. Forewords by Steven Spielberg and Francis Ford Coppola. New York: Abrams, 1997. Hardback, 232 pages, $39.95. A coffee-table book that tells you everything you want to know about George Lucas: his life, the films, Skywalker Ranch, and his movie business ventures.

Indiana Jones and the Last Crusade: Original Movie Script from The Movie Script Library (Premiere). The complete screenplay and movie stills. Recommended mostly for film buffs.

Indiana Jones and the Temple of Doom: The Illustrated Screenplay, by Willard Huyck and Gloria Katz, with introduction by Steven Spielberg. New York: Ballantine, 1984. Trade paperback, 122 pages, $17.95. Out of print. A great resource of images, storyboards, and the full text of the script, as well.

Raiders of the Lost Ark: The Illustrated Screenplay, by Lawrence Kasdan, with an introduction by Steven Spielberg. New York: Ballantine, 1981. Trade paperback, out of print. For a general reader, this provides the complete screenplay with more than two hundred selected storyboards, which breaks up the continuity of the script. Film buffs, of course, would prefer a text-only edition.

OTHER BOOKS OF INTEREST

From Eden to Exile: Unraveling Mysteries of the Bible, by Eric. H. Cline. Washington DC: National Geographic, 2007. Trade hardback, 256 pages, $26. In a review for *Booklist,* Ilene Cooper states that "what Cline intends here is a quick overview, a brisk trip through some of the great mysteries of biblical history, advancing his own theories about what happened and mentioning alternative opinions. . . . An accessibly written introduction that will likely prompt readers to dig deeper." Topics include: The Garden of Eden, Noah's Ark and the Flood, Sodom and Gomorrah's location, the dating of the Exodus, the Fall of Jericho, the Ark of the Covenant, and the Lost Tribes of Israel. Highly recommended.

The Worldwide Guide to Movie Locations: The Ultimate Travel Guide to Film Sites around the World, by Tony Reeves. London: Titan Books, 2006.

Trade paperback, 463 pages, $19.95. For any film buff, this book is your passport to the world of movie magic with "detailed coverage of over 1,500 films. Each listing contains information on the movie's key locations, along with travel details and a firsthand account of just exactly what the intrepid traveler can expect to find there."

The only book of its kind, it is definitive and generously illustrated with hundreds of black-and-white photographs of site locations. There's also a color section that highlights the geographical locations for some of the most popular movies in recent memory, including *The Lord of the Rings, Star Wars, Bridget Jones's* London, Harry Potter's England, and the world of James Bond. A treasure trove of information for fictional places you've probably only seen on the silver screen that, in fact, exist in the real world.

DVDS

Indiana Jones and the Raiders of the Lost Ark. Indian Jones and the Temple of Doom. Indiana Jones and the Last Crusade. Available in a boxed set with a disc of supplementary material, these are available in both widescreen and fullscreen (cropped; pan and scan), and have been digitally remastered and restored, so the colors are vibrant and the images sharp.

Indiana Jones Bonus Material. Packaged with the boxed set, this disc is three hours of supplementary material: original teasers and trailers; short featurettes on creating the sound, music, special effects, and stunts; and a film-by-film behind-the-scenes look explaining what they did and how they did it.

Indyfans: The Quest for Fortune and Glory, directed by Brandon Kleya, from Red Dot Film Studios (www.reddotfilmstudios.com). The first documentary by Indy fans *for* Indy fans, this independent production features "interviews with Indy fans, crew members, and cast from all over the globe, documenting stories about the impression the Indiana Jones films have made on their lives." The director, who has one of the largest collections of Indy memorabilia in the world, hopes to release this on DVD in May 2008—just in time for the release of the fourth Indiana Jones movie. I, for one, am looking forward to it!

A massive, detailed façade flanking the amphitheater that showcases the Stunt Spectacular. (Indiana Jones Stunt Spectacular, Walt Disney World, Orlando, Florida)

WEBSITES

HarrisonFordweb.com is a fan website established in 1999 that does an excellent job covering the comings and goings of Harrison Ford. Not surprisingly, most of the current coverage is centered on the fourth Indiana Jones movie.

IndianaJones.com is the official website. As such, it's big on marketing *Indiana Jones and the Kingdom of the Crystal Skull*, but devotes little space to previously released product. Even so, there's good material: downloadable photos, videos, screensavers, and breaking news (which is immediately repeated on the fan websites). This should be your first stop on the Web.

Magnoliprops.com is an Indy fan's version of Heaven created by Anthony "Indy" Magnoli. He picked up his distinctive nickname when, as a indigent student pursuing his archaeology degree at the University of

New Mexico, he was unable to buy the licensed prop replicas and so decided to make them himself. As it turned out, he was quite skilled at creating these replicas, which were made for his own collection; though he later produced replicas for independent films and theater productions. Magnoli's work, obviously of professional caliber, shows an extraordinary attention to detail and craftsmanship.

A long-time Indy fan now living in New Zealand, Magnoli explains a little about his background: "My father was a teacher obsessed with history. That, coupled with the Indy films, had a great effect on my love of archaeology and history. I received my first fedora when I was thirteen; and when I started going to college, I never went anywhere without that hat. I particularly love vintage-style clothing and apparel, which in part stemmed from my interest in the Indy films. *Raiders* will always be the original, full of magic and excitement, but my great affection for Grail lore puts *The Last Crusade* almost on par with it."

Explaining his methodology in constructing replicas, Magnoli explains:

> As for making any particular prop, one of the most impor-tant things involved is research. In the case of replicating something seen on screen, one of the first choices to make is whether to replicate the prop or the real-life object. For example, do you want a resin Grail or a clay Grail? Should Henry Jones's Grail Diary have repeated pages and random text, or should the book be readable like a real journal? The Headpiece to the Staff of Ra is a "worthless bronze medallion" (as Indy tells Marion in *Raiders*), yet the original prop was finished in a gold tone. Either way, realism is key. One of the best ways to give a prop the look of authenticity is proper antiquing. This is achieved with many methods, ranging from the use of strong, black coffee to stain paper to heavy use of sandpaper or, in some cases, actual physical abuse.

The prop replicas created by Magnoli were originally in the following Indiana Jones movies:

The Young Indiana Jones Chronicles
Indiana Jones's diary, Indiana Jones's passport (circa 1934), Young

Indiana Jones's passport (circa 1916), treasure map to the Peacock's Eye, reproduction photographs, a blank Indiana Jones diary, and Indiana Jones's diary inserts (replica photographs and documents).

Raiders of the Lost Ark

Golden Idol of Fertility, Ark of the Covenant (1:4 scale), Headpiece to the staff of Ra, Nazi Headpiece to the staff of Ra, Indy's pocket knife, Raider's map to the Chachapoyan temple, artifacts from Tec'na'al, Raider's sandbag, Belloq's passport, Indy's Bible page, Raider's journal, *Archaeological Review* article, Raiders torch, Toht's coat hanger, China Clipper ticket, Toht's *Life* magazine, U.S. Intel's German communiqué report, and Belloq's floor plan to the map room.

Temple of Doom

Lao Che's diamond, Lao Che's gold coins, Indy's Eye of Horus cuff links, Sankara Stones (Sivalinga), Sankara Sanskrit manuscripts, Indiana Jones voodoo doll, and an *Archaeological Review* article.

The fabled Eye of Mara found in the "Temple of the Forbidden Eye."
(Indiana Jones Adventure—"The Eye of Mara," Disneyland, Anaheim, California)

The Last Crusade

Henry Jones Sr.'s Grail diary, Grail diary prop replica, the Cross of Coronado, a ceramic Holy Grail cup, a fragment of the Grail tablet, a medieval Grail Knight painting, a medieval crucifixion painting, magnifying glass from Indy's desk, Henry Jones Sr.'s passport, a Henry Jones travel document, a Nazi "Wanted" flyer (for Dr. Jones Sr.), Henry Jones's ID card, a Nazi "Wanted" flyer (for Dr. Jones Jr.—but don't call him "Junior"), Indy's ID card and driver's license, a Brotherhood of the Cruciform pin, a Zeppelin ticket, a Nazi telegram sent to antiquities collector Walter Donovan, an article from *Archaeological Review,* a blank Grail diary, Grail diary inserts, and a Grail tablet rubbing.

NOTE: All the photographs of prop replicas in this book are from this website.

Starwars.com is the official *Star Wars* shop, so Indy fans will have to know where to look to find the Indy stuff. The easiest way to reach the Indy-only merchandise is to use the drop-down menu for "Shop by Category" and choose "Indiana Jones." Currently, the selection is anemic, with only two pages of offerings (DVDs, baseball caps, fedoras, and T-shirts), but it's all reasonably priced. Expect to see a flood of Indy product by April 2008.

TheRaider.net is the *best* Indy Jones site on the Web. The news section is frequently updated and its separate sections (the films, research, and features) have a lot to offer Indy fans, new and old alike. You could spend hours exploring this site, which is exhaustive, definitive, and fun to browse.

throwmetheidol.com is the most complete fan website that details all the various Indy Jones collectibles over the years. The coverage of related collectibles tied into the release of the fourth movie is extensive and impressive.

YoungIndy.com is the official website for *The Adventures of Young Indiana Jones,* which should see a resurgence of interest, especially with the long-awaited release of the DVDs.

MEMORABILIA AND COLLECTIBLES

eBay.com is the biggest flea market in the world, truly a bazaar of the bizarre! As such, the selection of Indiana Jones stuff is mind-boggling: costumes, action figures, games, DVDs, VHS videos, toys, and movie prop replicas.

Unfortunately, movie memorabilia on eBay—unless you're buying from a trusted source—is a potential nightmare, since forged signatures are commonplace, and shady merchants offer dubious "certificates of authenticity" to bolster their inflated claims. Unless you know and trust the seller, keep in mind that the signed photograph/bound script/movie poster is likely to be a forgery.

As famous author J. K. Rowling explained on her website regarding eBay, "As far as I could tell on the day I dropped in, only *one* [italics mine] of the signatures on offer appeared genuine. There seems to be a lot of people out there trying to con Harry Potter fans. . . . So it remains for me to warn you personally: 'bonded certificates of authenticity' do not guarantee that I have ever been on the same continent of the book in question, let alone signed it."

The same obviously applies to signed Harrison Ford memorabilia.

Sideshowtoy.com, the premiere seller of busts, statues, and other movie-related collectibles, is bringing out a line of Indiana Jones product from all four films in the form of "twelve-inch figures, premium format figures, and life-size busts that will range in price from $69.99 to $599.99." (I'm looking forward to getting my hands on Willie Scott's bust.)

LICENSEES FOR THE FOURTH MOVIE

Perhaps tapping into the Force, Howard Roffman, president of Lucas Licensing, remarked that "it's been nineteen years since the last film and we are sensing a huge pent-up demand for everything Indy."

Here's what's available.

Gentle Giant is in the early stages of designing its line of statues and busts, which includes Indy firing his pistol while riding a horse, Indy and his father in the German motorcycle with sidecar, and a bust of Indy (sans hat). A figurine exclusive to the Disney theme parks is a seven-inch Indiana Jones with bullwhip and pistol in hand. Indy is standing on part of an ancient ruin and comes with accessories, including a Grail diary, a golden idol, and a sword.

Hallmark has developed a line of greeting cards, party goods, and ornaments. No details available at press time.

Hasbro has a line of figurines intended for smaller children. The "Adventure Hero 2-packs" include product from the first movie: Indy with whip in hand while holding the golden idol, the Nazi mechanic who engages Indy in a fistfight near the flying wing aircraft, Indy with pistol and whip in hand, the menacing Egyptian swordsman dressed in black, Sallah holding a torch, a mummy-like figure with a snake wrapped around its torso, a ghostly creature, the Ark of the Covenant, and Dr. Belloq in Jewish ceremonial gear.

Larger, more detailed pieces (3-3/4 inch) show five figures with accessories: Indy holding his pistol and the golden idol, the Egyptian swordsman dressed in black, the Egyptian collaborator who aids the Nazis, Dr. Belloq in full ceremonial garb when opening the Ark, and Marion Ravenwood wearing a white blouse and red pants.

Lego is launching play sets, with some based on the first movie and others based on the fourth movie, ranging in price from $9.99 to $79.99. The play sets for the previously released movies include: "Temple Escape" (the rolling boulder scene, spiders, and poison dart) for $49.99; "Race for the Stolen Treasure" (two desert vehicles in the chase scene during the road march) for $29.99; "Indiana Jones and the Lost Tomb" (Indy rescues Marion from snakes in an Egyptian tomb) for $19.99; and the "Motorcycle Chase" (Indy and his father escape on the motorcycle with sidecar) for $9.99. Play sets tied to *Crystal Skull* include: "Jungle Duel" and "Temple of the Crystal Skull."

LucasArts has announced the release of its Indiana Jones interactive video games for use on the PlayStation 3 and Xbox 360 platforms. (No details were available at press time.)

Official Pix (officialpix.com) offers a line of color photographs from the Indiana Jones movies. Printed on glossy Fujifilm archival paper, the photos bear a one-inch round prismatic Indiana Jones sticker that clearly identifies them as licensed product.

Given that eBay is a bootlegger's market where scum gather to sell forged signatures and rescanned photos, the great benefit of buying a picture from this company is that you can be sure it's the real deal.

A full line of 11 x 14-inch color stills from *Indiana Jones and the Kingdom of the Crystal Skull* is in the works. The first picture, limited to 250 hand-numbered copies, retails for $19.99; it sold out soon after it was announced. The photo showed Harrison Ford in costume, relaxing in a director's chair between scene takes. Harrison is clearly older, presumably wiser, and looks every inch the intrepid explorer that is Indiana Jones.

Random House, Scholastic, and **DK Publishing** have issued a line of books, including movie tie-in editions and overview titles. Two titles will be of great interest to Indy fans:

The Complete Making of Indiana Jones, by J. W. Rinzler and Laurent Bouzereau. New York: Random House, 2008. Trade hardback, 288 pages. Intended for adults, this is a movie-by-movie look at all four films with "a behind-the-scenes look at the people, places, technology, and events that went into the creation of all four *Indiana Jones* movies." It does not include any coverage of *The Young Indiana Jones Chronicles.*

Indiana Jones: The Ultimate Guide, by DK Publishing, London, 2008. Hardcover, 144 pages, for ages 9–12. As with all DK products, this is in full color and beautifully designed with lots of visual interest. A good overview for old and new fans alike.

Sideshow Toy offers a line of collectibles: figurines (twelve-inch and larger) and busts, ranging in price from $69.99 for the twelve-inches up to $599.99 for the high-end product. As I've got several of their pieces from the *Lord of the Rings* line, I can highly recommend this company. The products are of outstanding quality and priced so they are affordable to even the casual collector.

Topps Company is issuing ninety cards with a retro theme: scenes from the first three movies that comprise the "Indiana Jones Heritage" card collection. Topps, which had previously issued "Raiders of the Lost Ark" cards in 1981, is upping the ante the second time around by hoping to secure signatures from the films' principal actors, including Michael Byrne (as Colonel Vogel, film 3), Kate Capshaw (as Willie Scott, film 2), Denholm Elliot (as Marcus Brody, films 1–3; "1/1 cut signature card"), Harrison Ford (as Indy, films 1–4), screenwriter Lawrence Kasdan, producer Kathleen Kennedy, executive producer George Lucas, producer Frank Marshall, Alfred Molina (as Satipo, film 1), Pat Roach (in four roles, films 1–3; "1/1 cut signature card"), director Steven Spielberg, and David Yip (as Wu Han, film 2).

As befitting a retro-designed card set, a stick of gum will be included in each card pack. In addition, "parallel" cards and "sketch" cards (original art drawn on special cardstock) will be randomly inserted.

Ira Friedman, Topps's vice president of publishing, observed that "Our 'Heritage' treatment for the original movies is a nostalgic and fun way to kick off our *Indiana Jones* trading card initiative. We're certain the core fans will treasure this early appetizer, the first phase of an ongoing program that will transition to the new movie and beyond."

Cards for the "Heritage" card set were issued in February 2008; that set is followed by a card set from the fourth movie to be released in May 2008.

Toynami has a twenty-four-inch cinemaquette that uses a silicon sculpting process to achieve a superior likeness for its line of high-end collectibles, likely limited to one thousand pieces. "Indiana Jones: Raiders of the Lost Ark" shows Indy with bullwhip in hand, dressed in his field outfit. The cost may be up to $1,500.

An enigmatic mask greets visitors to Adventureland. (Magic Kingdom, Walt Disney World, Orlando, Florida)

ACKNOWLEDGMENTS

Writing a book is like going on an expedition, and as with any expedition, success hinges on whether or not you've got the right team assembled. In this case, I was fortunate to have my steadfast friend, **Tim Kirk,** who has illustrated all of my previous books published at Hampton Roads Publishing. On this outing to places unknown, Tim got to work well before the "expedition" got underway, with detailed information about archaeology, suggesting websites, mailing newspaper clippings, making phone calls, and offering information about his contributions as a Disney Imagineer who worked on several Indiana Jones–themed projects at Disney's theme parks. Tim allowed me to go through his art files and select some little-seen pieces of art that we thought would look good in this book; he also drew pen-and-ink illustrations especially for me. I am, as always, deeply in his debt. Thank you, Tim, your help is always appreciated.

I am likewise indebted to **Anthony "Indy" Magnoli,** who generously allowed me to reproduce the photographs he took of his prop replicas collection. Once a college student majoring in archaeology, Anthony couldn't afford to buy the existing prop replicas and so decided to make his own. The result is a personal collection—no pieces for sale, of course—of professional quality replicas of key artifacts from the Indiana Jones movies, and other movies as well. (Anthony now makes a *very* good living, down in New Zealand, making period clothing from the 1930s and '40s for his discerning male clientele worldwide.)

Dr. Eric H. Cline earns the Golden Shovel Award for taking time out of his hectic schedule as an archaeology professor at George Washington University to lend a hand. He allowed me to reprint what I think is an eye-opening and thought-provoking article, humorously titled "Raiders of the Faux Ark"; wrote an introduction especially for this book; allowed himself to be interviewed for an article to explain what a field archaeologist does; and then read the working manuscript to provide much-needed feedback, which improved this book's contents. Thank you, Eric, for taking the time to lend your voice and expertise to this project.

At Hampton Roads Publishing, I'd like to thank the following fine folks: my editor and old pal, **Robert S. Friedman;** CEO and older pal, **Jack Jennings;** art director **Jane Hagaman;** and editrix **Tania Seymour,** who sees more in my books than I ever do. I am deeply indebted to **Steve Amarillo,** whose imaginative book design greatly enhanced its textual and visual appeal.

Finally, I'd like to thank my long-suffering wife **Mary,** who really is the biggest Indiana Jones fan I know on the planet. For years she's complained that she's waited long enough for the fourth film, which is true enough; I hope this book can tide her over until the May 2008 release of *Indiana Jones and the Kingdom of the Crystal Skull,* for which she'll be present on opening day at the first showing here in town.

Thanks, finally, to every one of you readers who decided to go on this expedition with us. I surely could not have asked for better company.

THE MEMBERS OF
THIS EXPEDITION

GEORGE BEAHM has never scaled the Seven Sisters, nor has he HALO-ed, and he most assuredly has never explored the undersea world discovered by Jacques Cousteau. An armchair traveler who enjoys his creature comforts, George has published more than thirty books, mostly on popular culture. A former field artillery officer, George is a book industry expert who has worked as a self-publisher, regional publisher, author, marketing director, designer, packager, and marketing consultant. He lives with his wife Mary in Williamsburg, Virginia. His website is at www.stealthe book.com.

TIM KIRK is a designer with extensive experience in a broad media spectrum—from book and magazine illustration to theme park and museum exhibit design. Tim's paintings based on J. R. R. Tolkien's epic fantasy *The Lord of the Rings* appeared in the *1975 Tolkien Calendar,* published by Ballantine Books. His illustrations have appeared in a wide variety of books, magazines, and fanzines; he has produced artwork for greeting cards, comics, websites, jigsaw puzzles, costume designs, and character concepts for fantasy role-playing games. He is a five-time winner of the prestigious Hugo Award for science fiction illustration.

For 22 years, Tim was employed as an Imagineer by the Walt Disney Company. He contributed significantly to several major Disney theme park projects, including Epcot Center, Pleasure Island, the Disney-MGM Studio Tour (Florida), Disneyland (Anaheim), and Tokyo DisneySea— the second gated theme park for the Tokyo Disney Resort, which opened in 2001. Tim was lead concept designer and art director for the Indiana Jones scene in "The Great Movie Ride" at the Disney MGM Studios at Walt Disney World. Tim was also a concept designer for the Indiana Jones Stunt Theater and the Indiana Jones merchandise shop, both also at the

Disney MGM Studios. He was part of the concept team for "Indiana Jones and the Temple of the Crystal Skull," the anchor attraction for the Lost River Delta area at Tokyo DisneySea.

Tim was a concept artist on *The Haunted Mansion* (2003), a Disney feature film based on the theme park attraction of the same name. In partnership with his brother and sister-in-law (also Disney veterans), Tim created Kirk Design Incorporated in 2002 (www.kirkdesigninc.com). Kirk Design specializes in themed concept and exhibit design for museums, theme parks, restaurants, and retail outlets, with a strong emphasis on immersive, innovative storytelling; recently completed projects include the Science Fiction Museum and Hall of Fame in Seattle (2004), the Parsonage of Aimee Semple McPherson in Los Angeles (April 2006), and the Center for Water Education in Hemet, California (2007). Other clients include the Ronald Reagan Presidential Library, the Aquarium of the Pacific (Long Beach, California), and Ghirardelli Chocolate.

A third-generation southern California native, Tim Kirk is a graduate of California State University at Long Beach, with a master's degree in illustration. He and his wife, Linda, make their home in Long Beach. His website is at www.kirkdesigninc.com.

ANTHONY "INDY" MAGNOLI is the proprietor of Magnoli Clothiers. Specializing in men's clothing from the 1930s and '40s, Magnoli Clothiers services a worldwide clientele of discriminating customers who wish to dress for success. A skilled artisan, "Indy" got his start by creating one-of-a-kind prop replicas inspired by the Indiana Jones movies. He subsequently went on to create props from other popular movies and television shows, including *The Hobbit, The Lord of the Rings,* and *The X Files.* He lives in Wanganui, New Zealand. His websites are at www.magnoliprops.com and www.magnoliclothiers.com.

DR. ERIC H. CLINE is Chair of the Department of Classical and Semitic Languages and Literatures, Associate Professor of Classics and of Anthropology (Ancient History and Archaeology), and advisor to the undergraduate majors in archaeology at The George Washington University, where he has won both national and local teaching awards. A former Fulbright scholar with degrees from Dartmouth, Yale, and the

University of Pennsylvania, he is associate director (USA) of the ongoing excavations at Megiddo (biblical Armageddon) in Israel as well as co-director of the ongoing excavations at Tel Kabri, also located in Israel. An award-winning author, he is perhaps best known for his books *The Battles of Armageddon: Megiddo and the Jezreel Valley from the Bronze Age to the Nuclear Age* (2000) and *Jerusalem Besieged: From Ancient Canaan to Modern Israel* (2004). His most recent book is entitled *From Eden to Exile: Unraveling Mysteries of the Bible,* published by the National Geographic Society (June 2007). His website is at http://home.gwu/edu/~ehcline/.

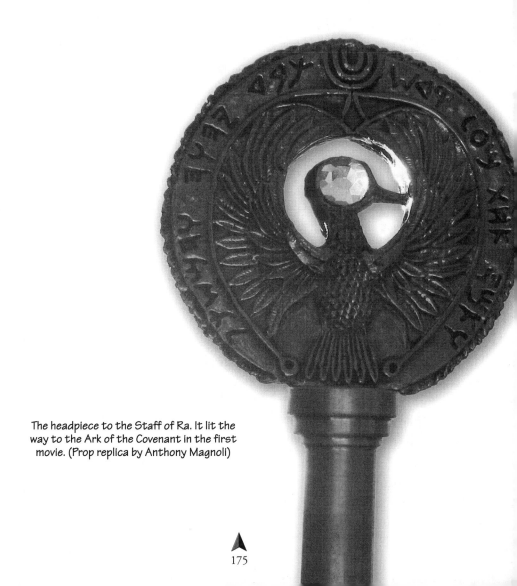

The headpiece to the Staff of Ra. It lit the way to the Ark of the Covenant in the first movie. (Prop replica by Anthony Magnoli)